Cut & Copy
creative clip art for...

Babies

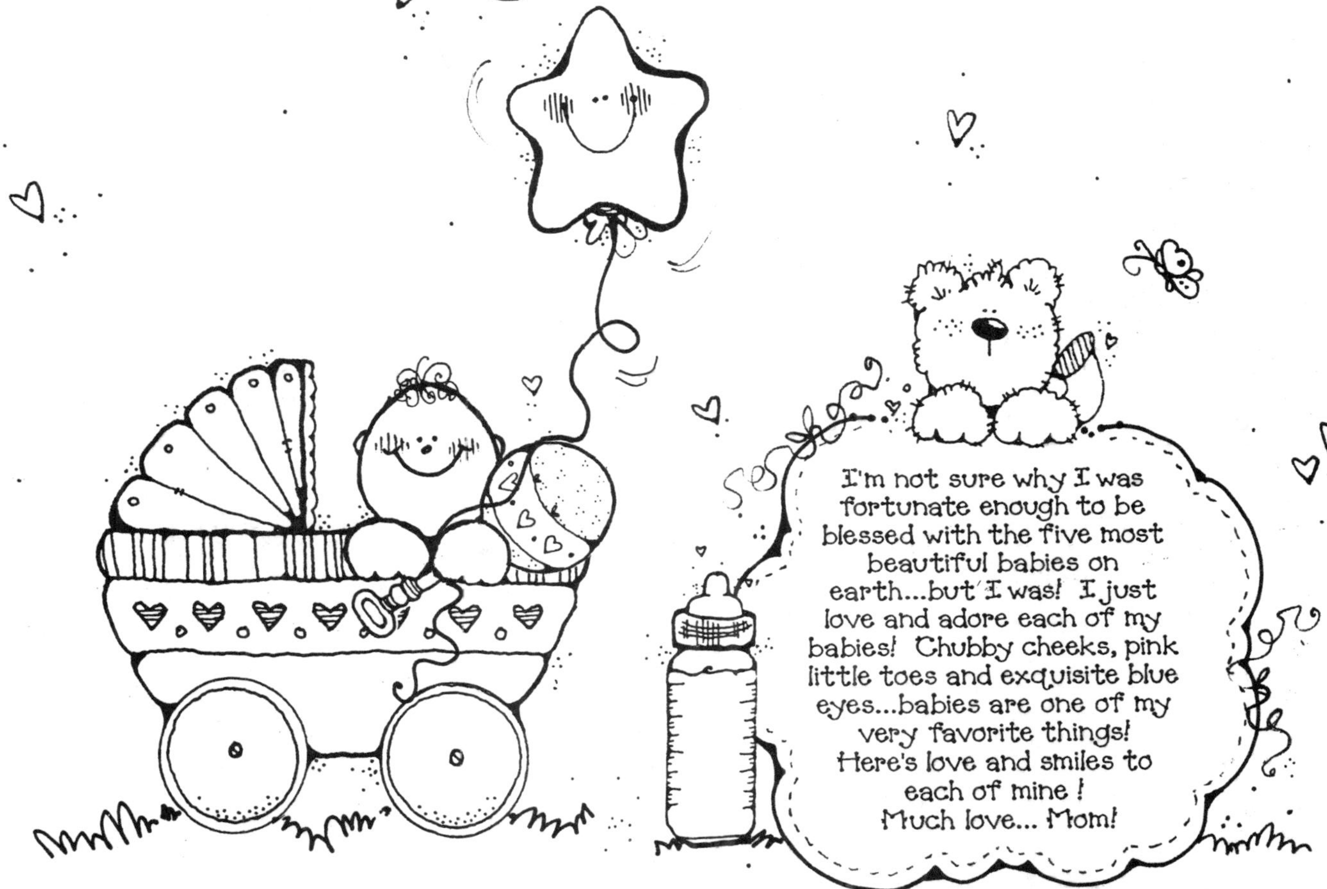

original designs by Dianne J. Hook

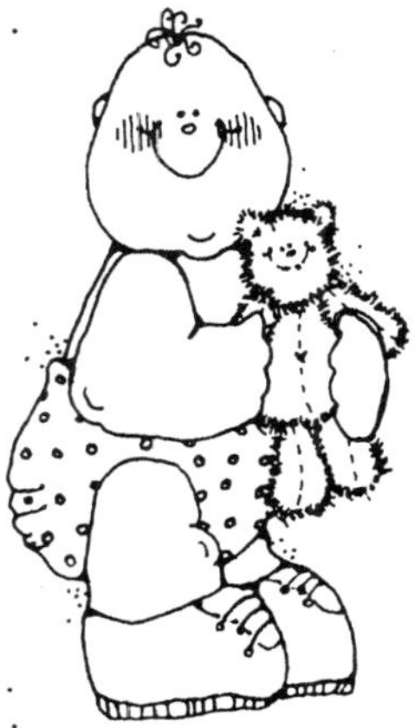

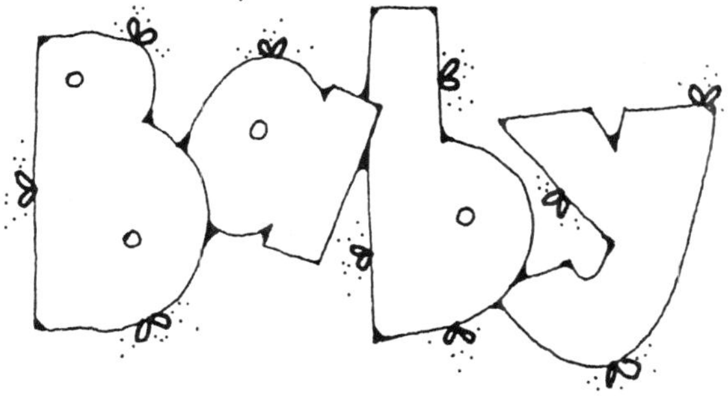

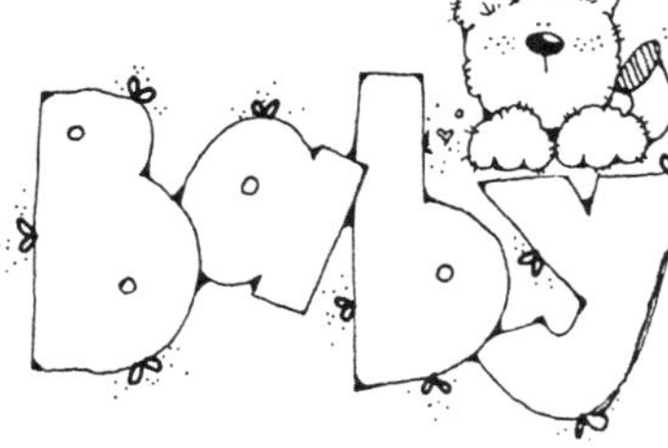

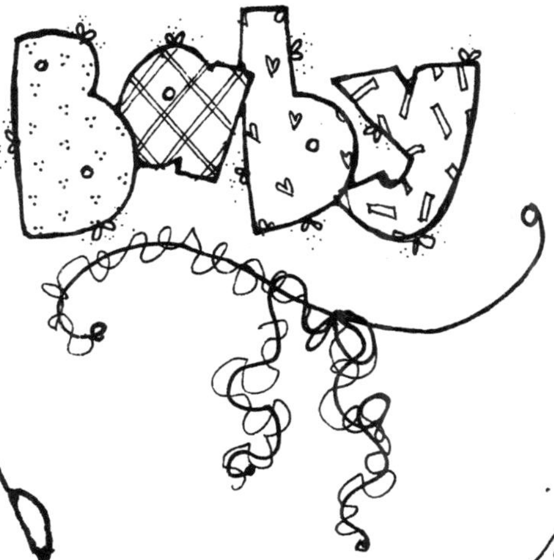

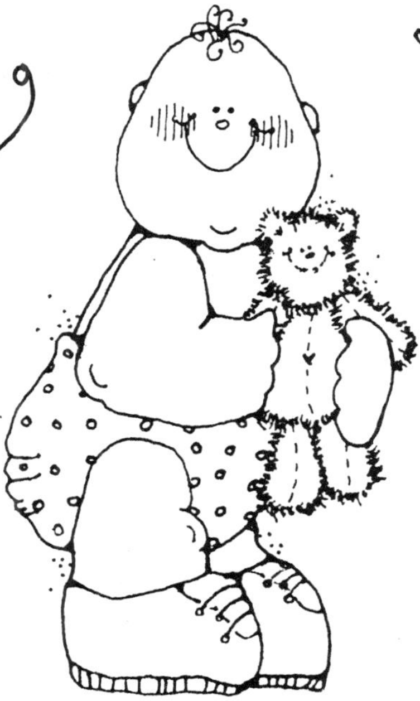

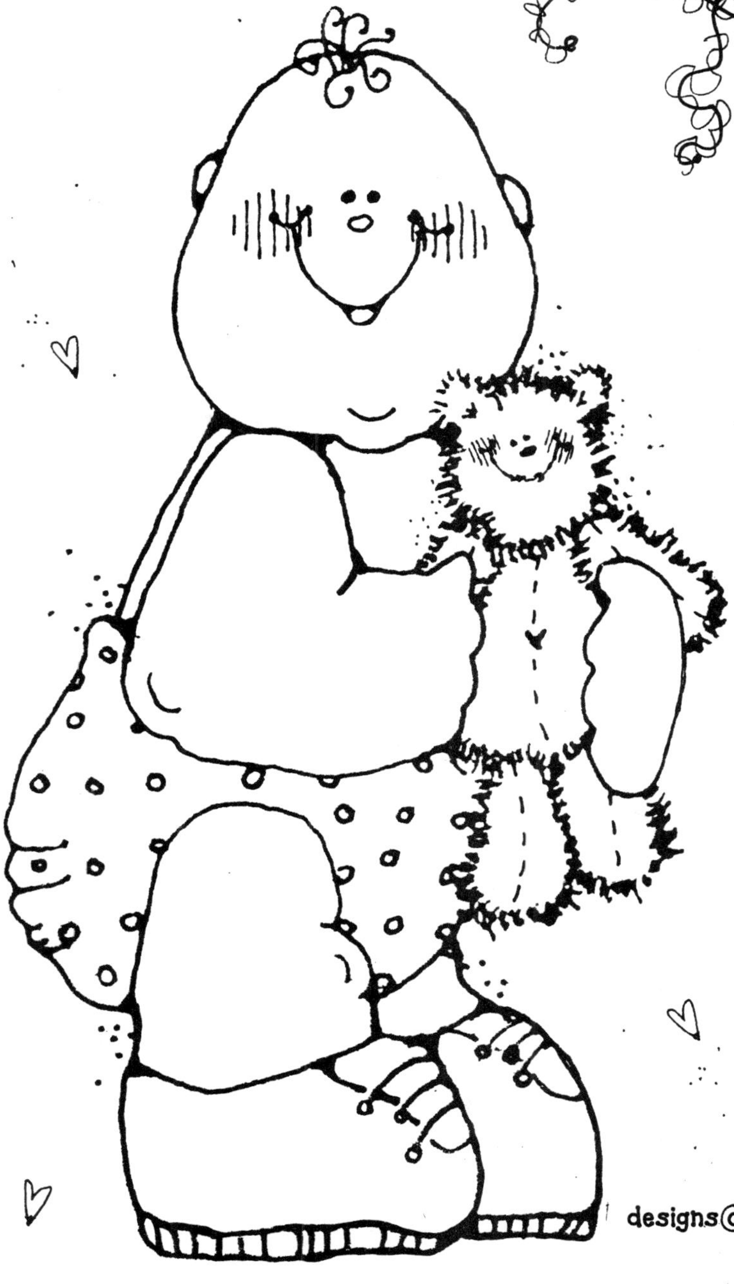

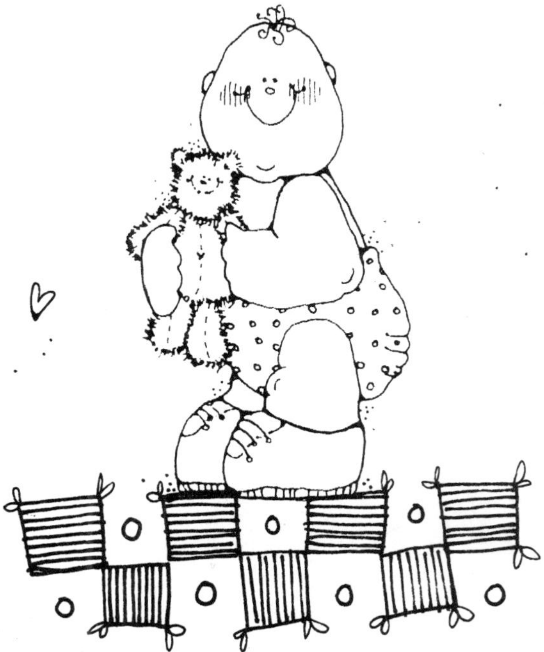

designs © dianne j. hook

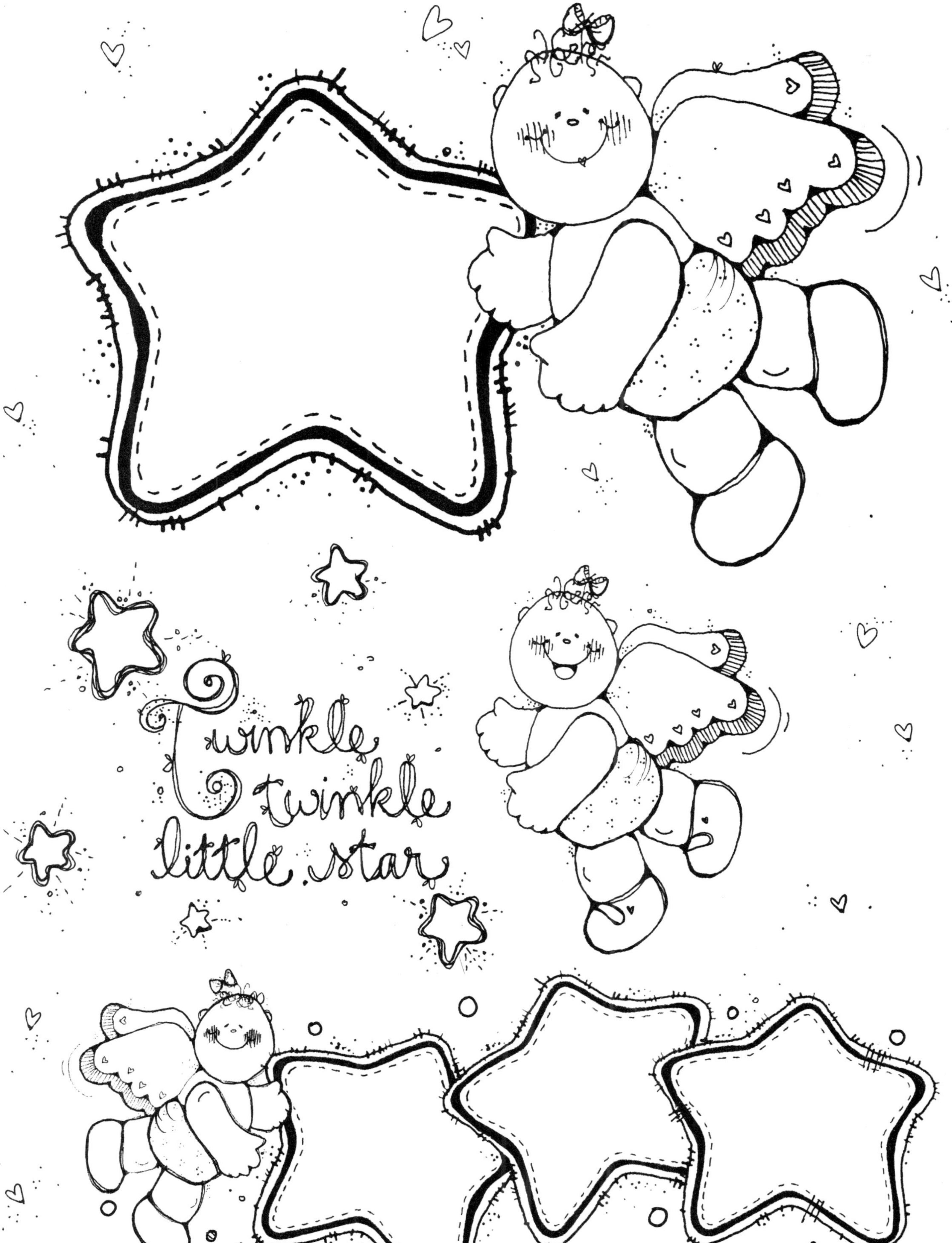
twinkle twinkle little star

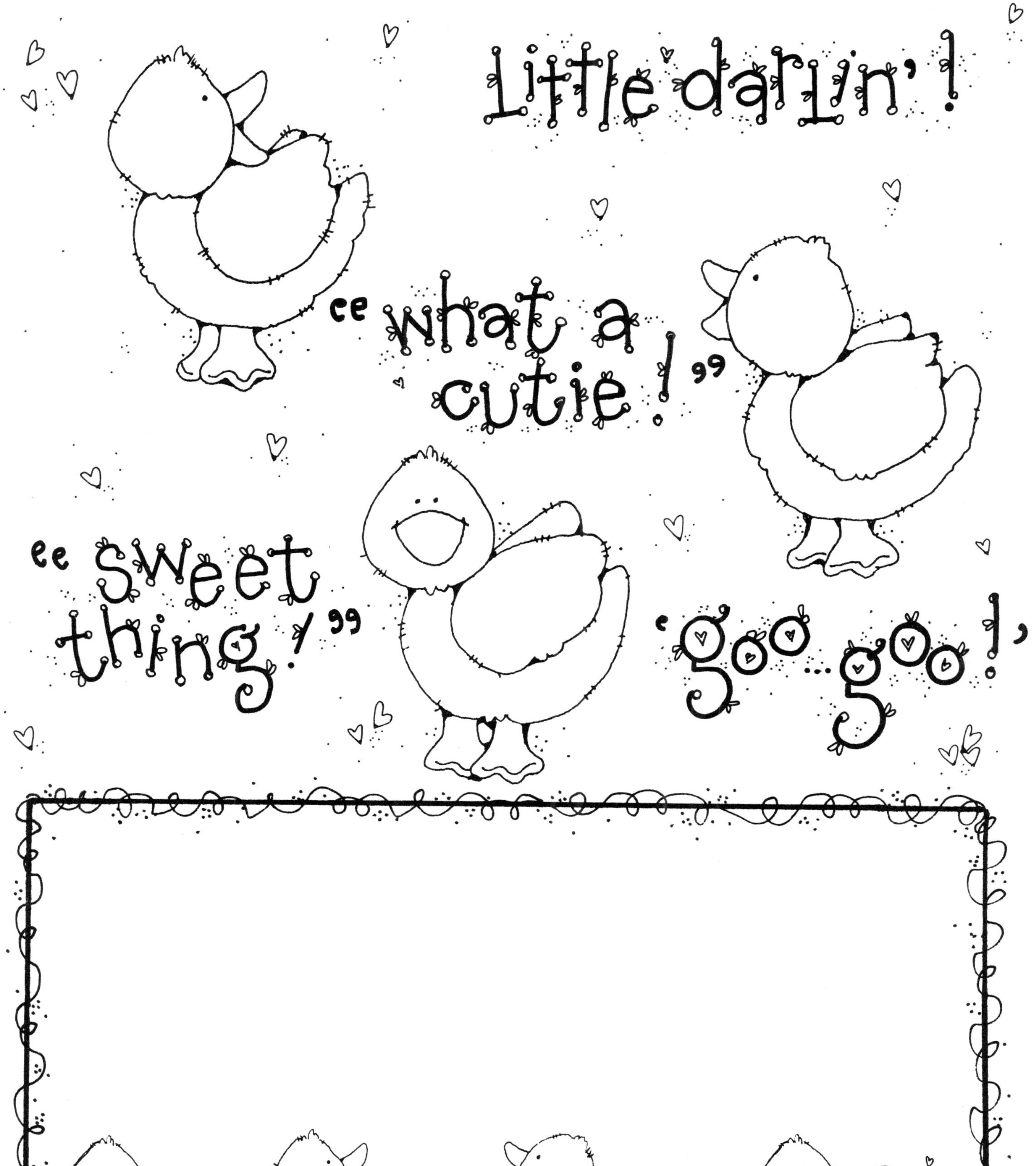
Little darlin'!
"what a cutie!"
"sweet thing!"
'goo...goo!'

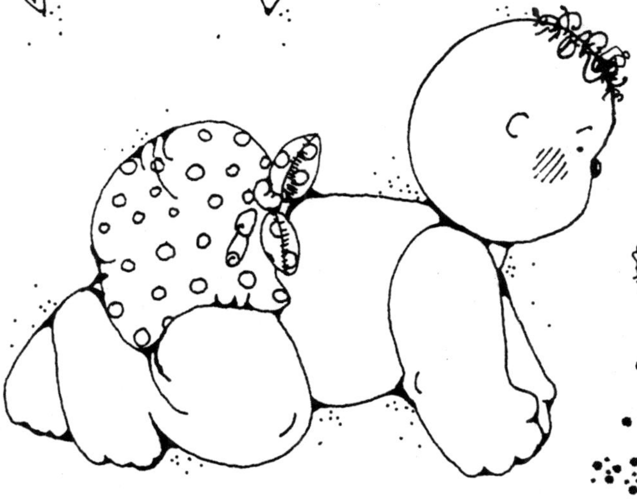

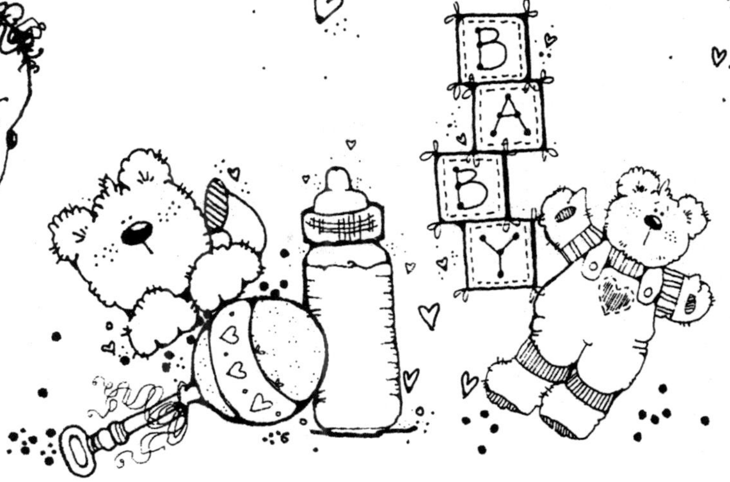

baby's first

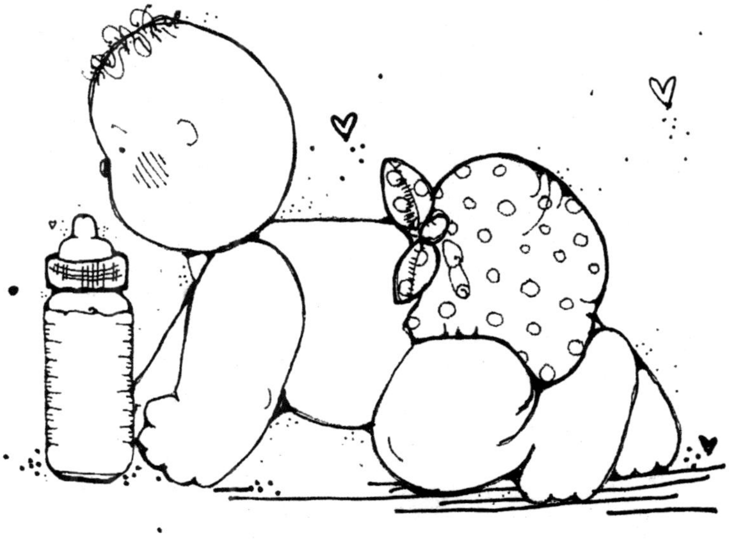

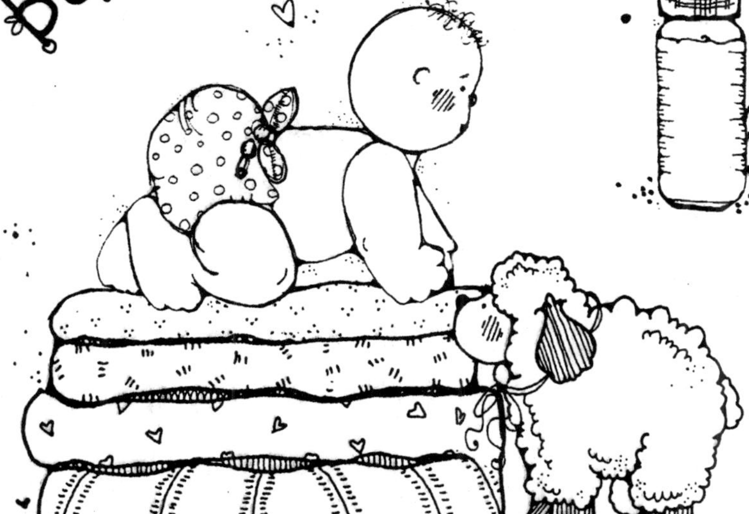

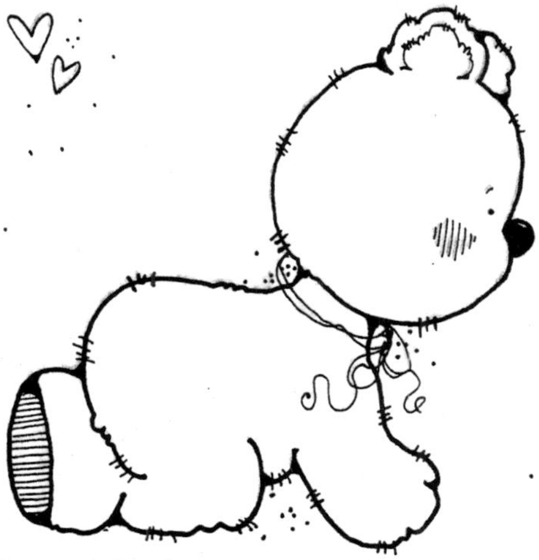

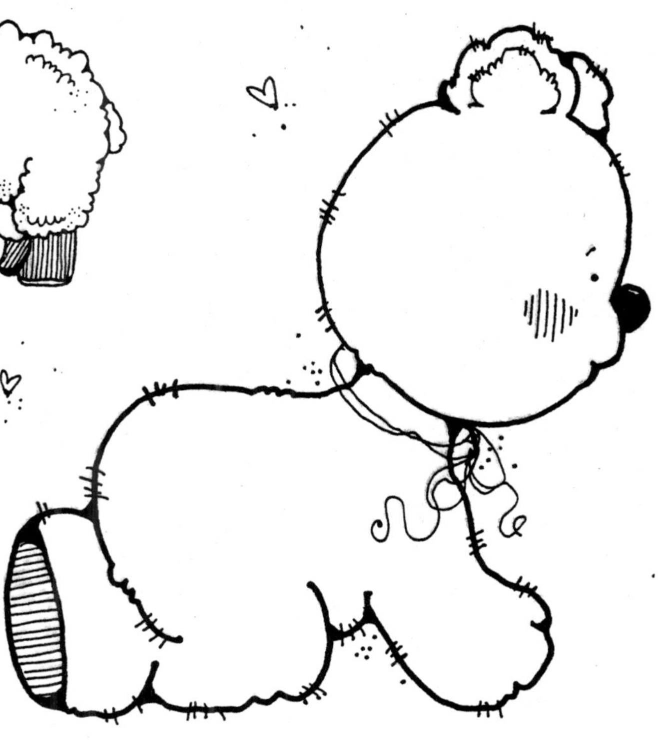

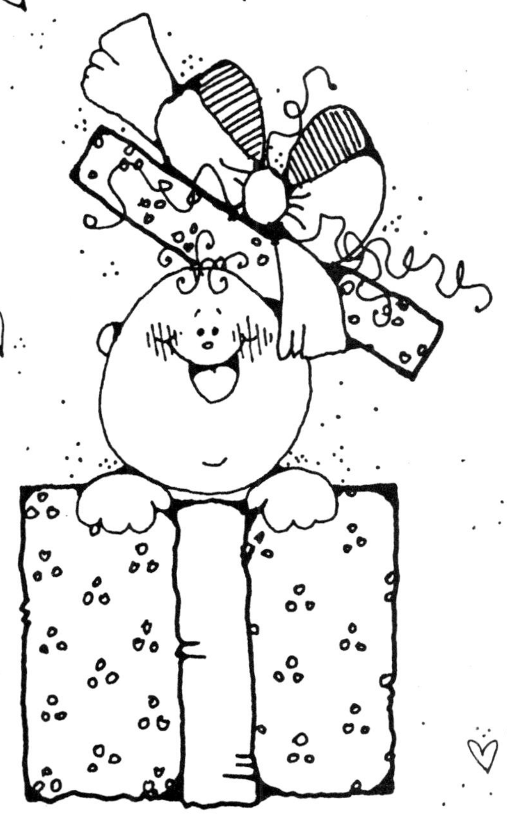

come to a Baby Shower!

date:
time:
place:
for:

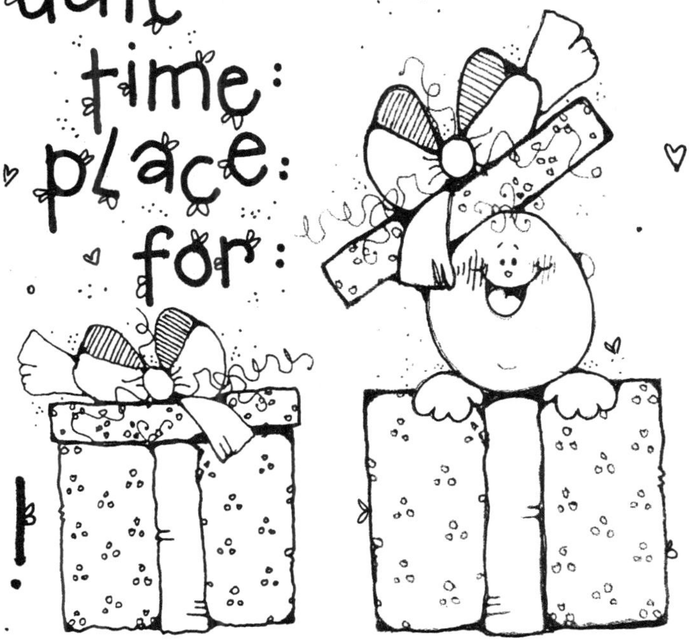

congratulations!

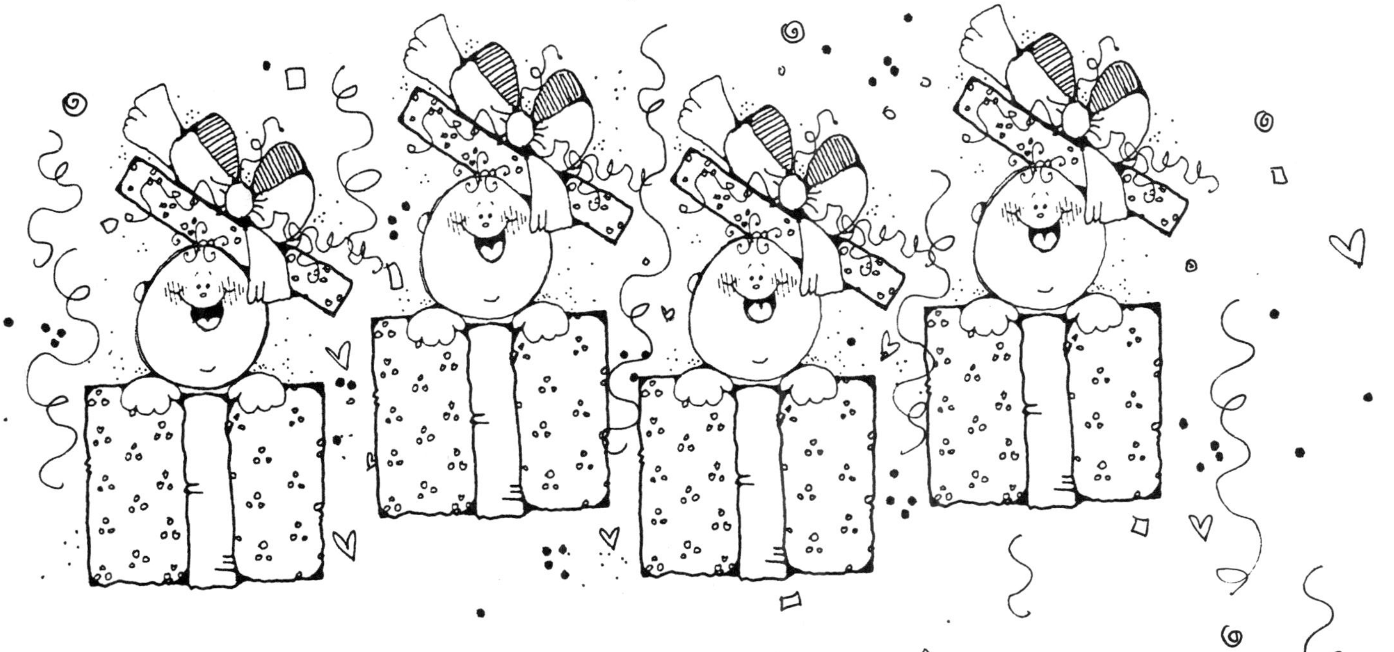

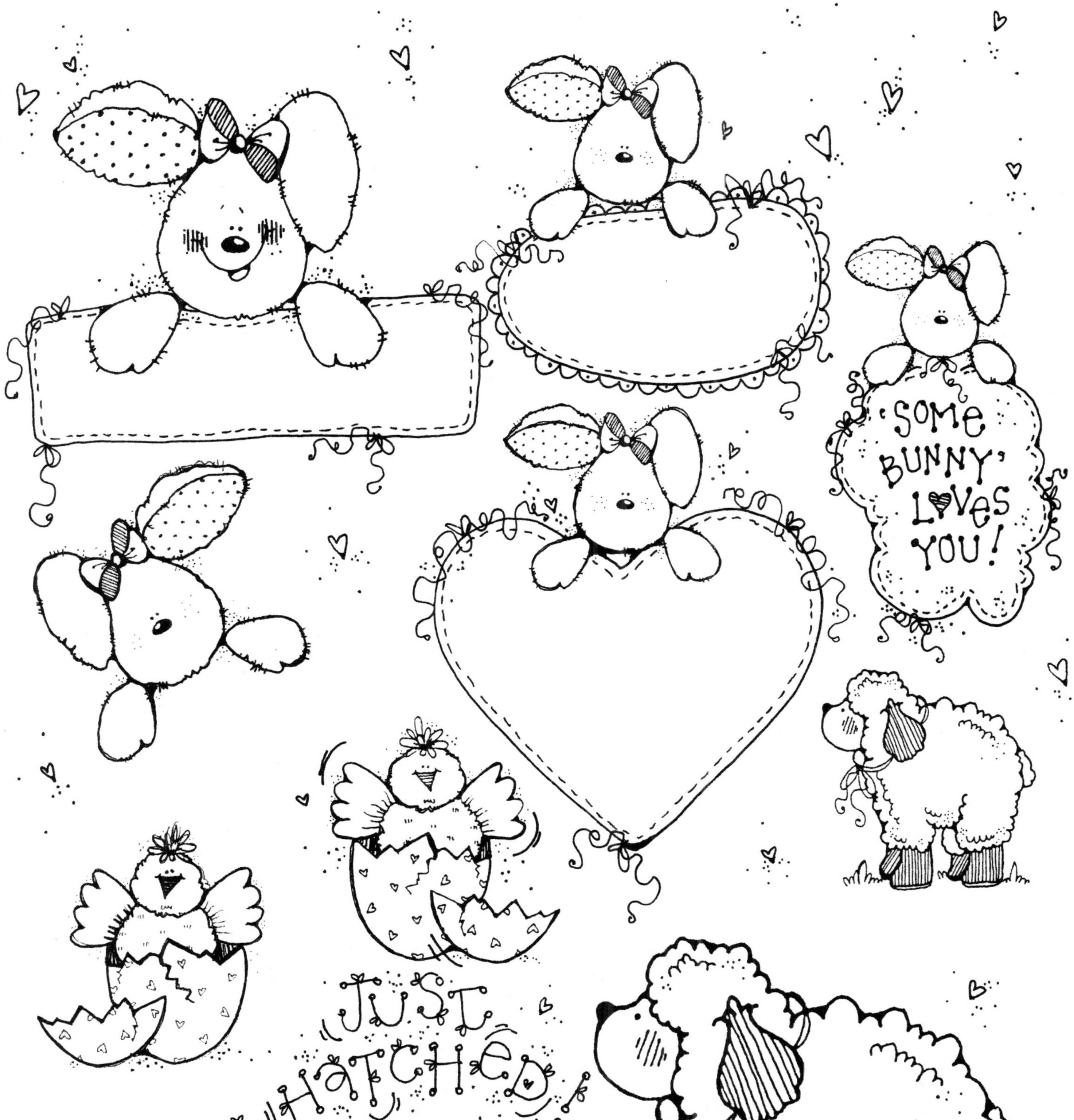
SOME BUNNY LOVES YOU!
JUST HATCHED!

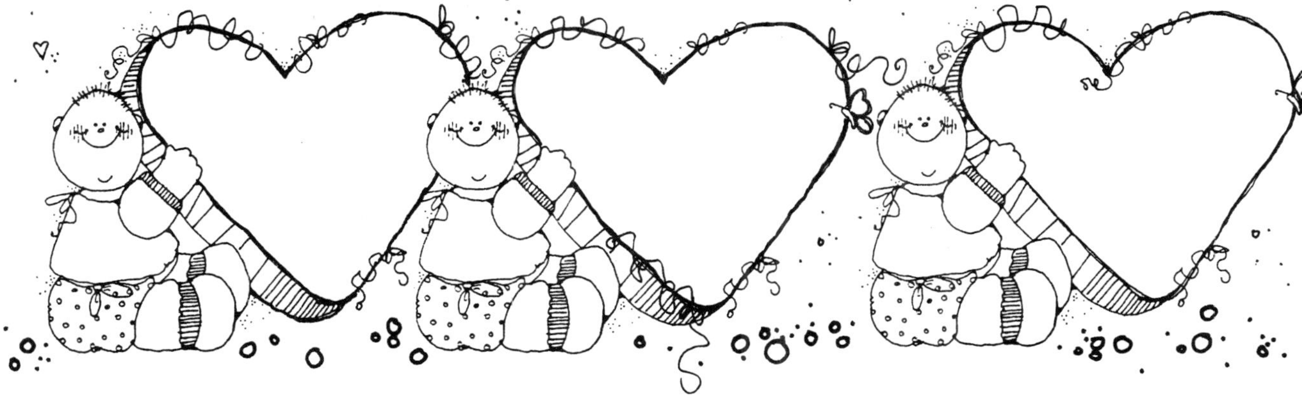

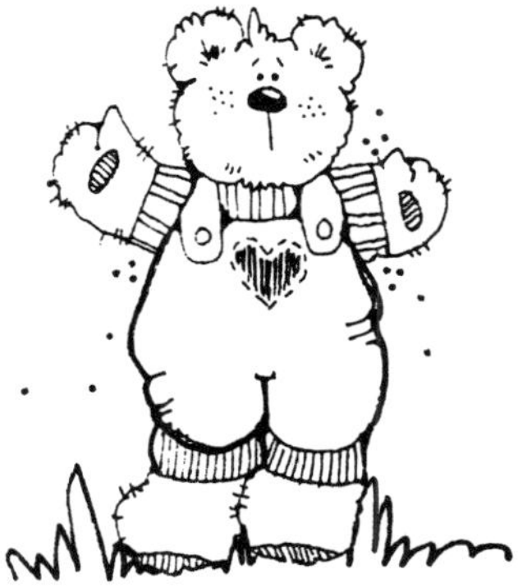

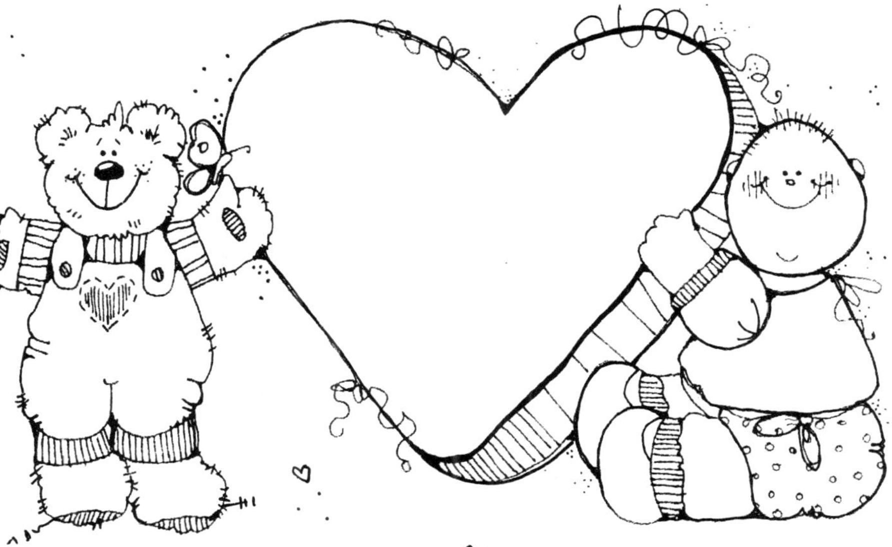

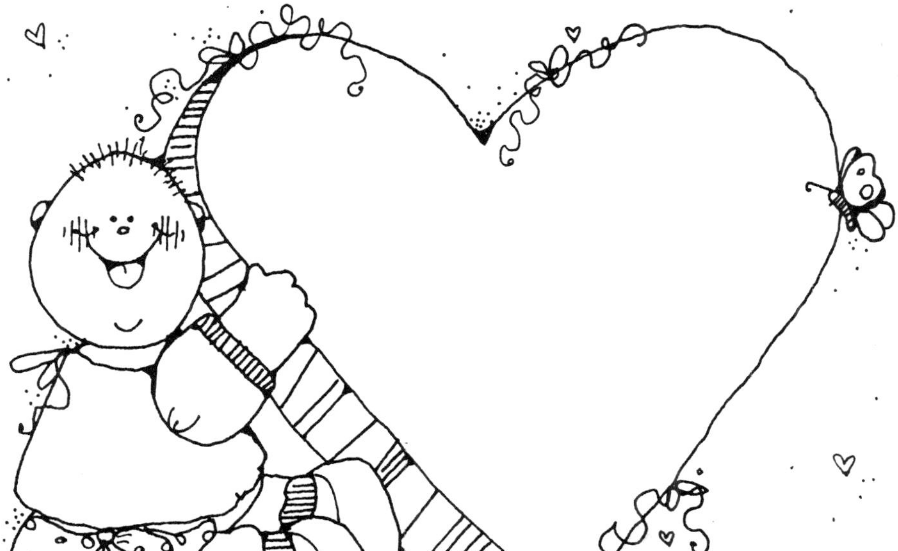

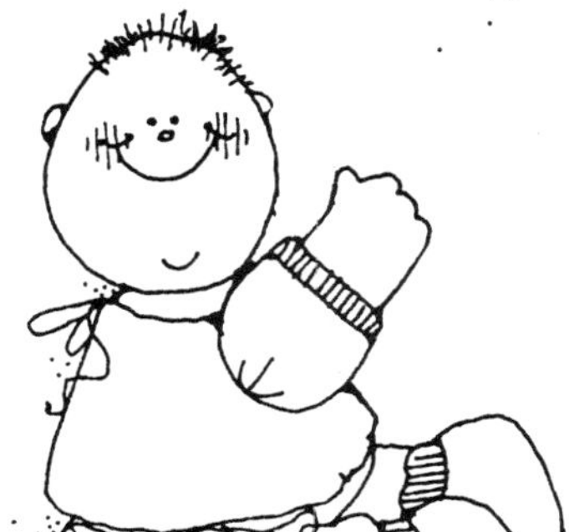

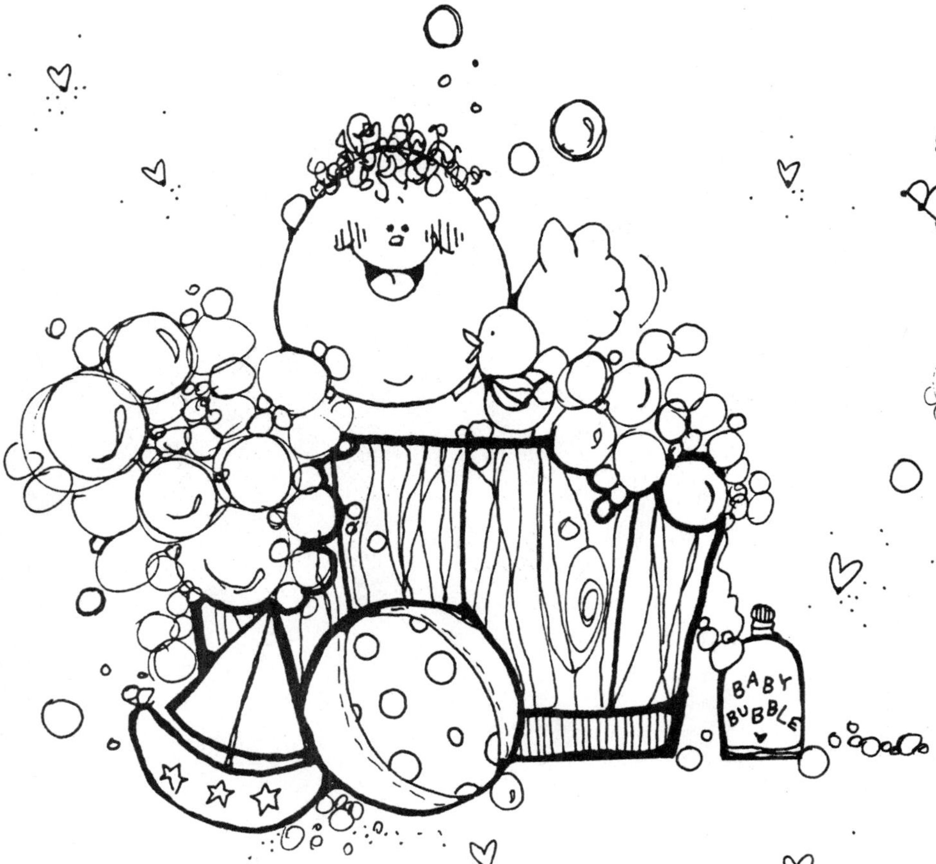

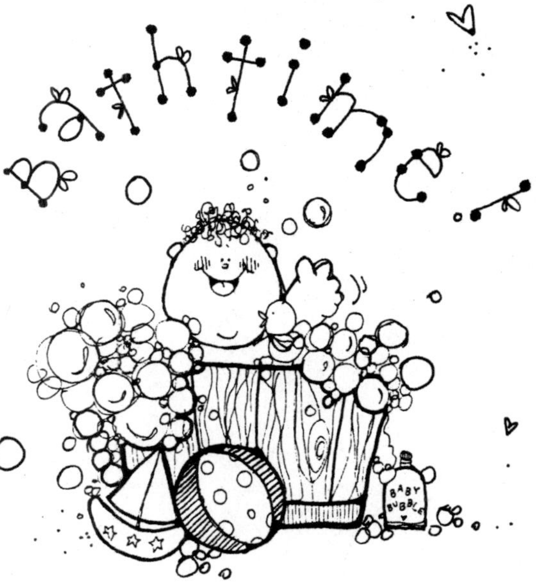

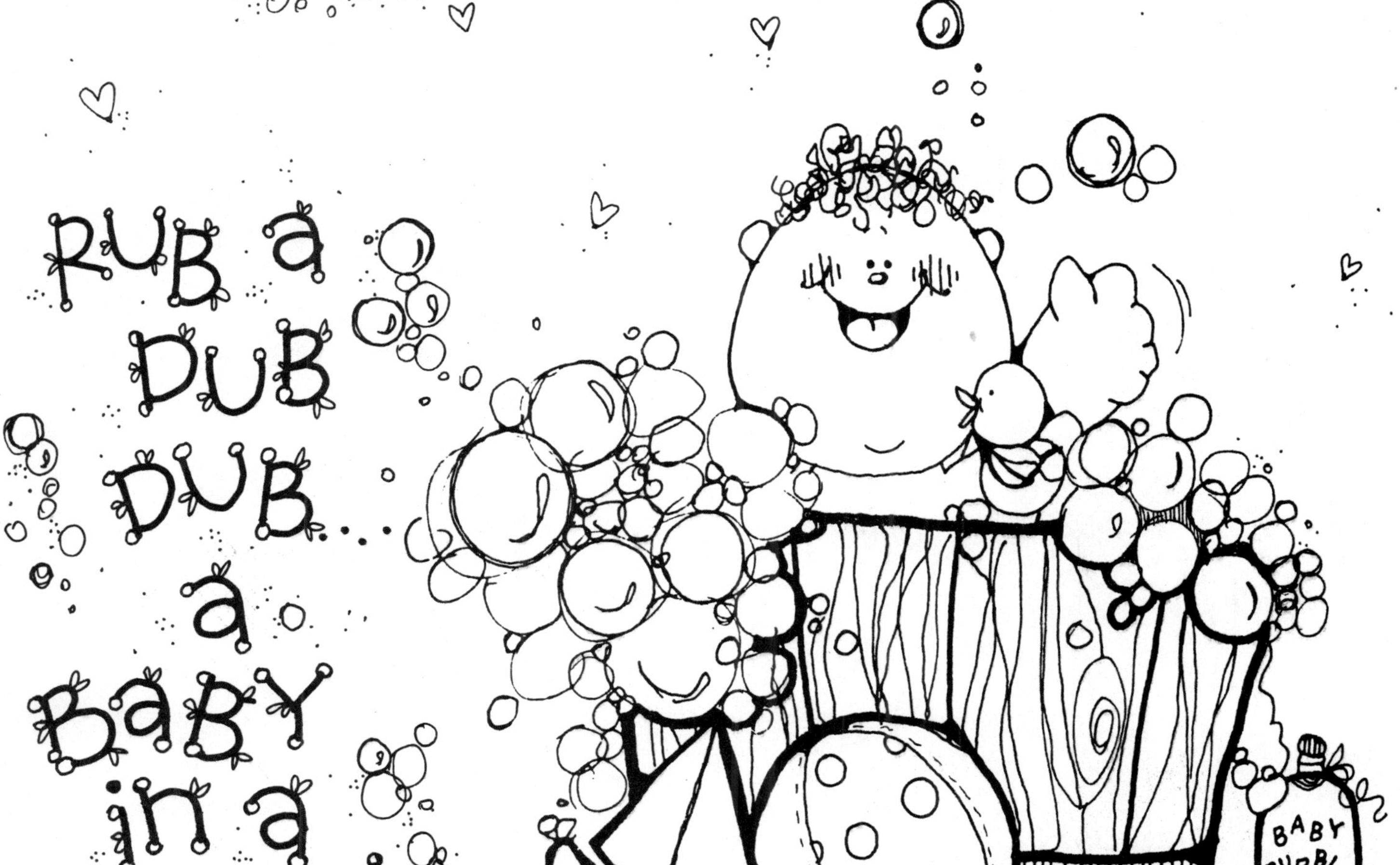

designs©dianne j. hook

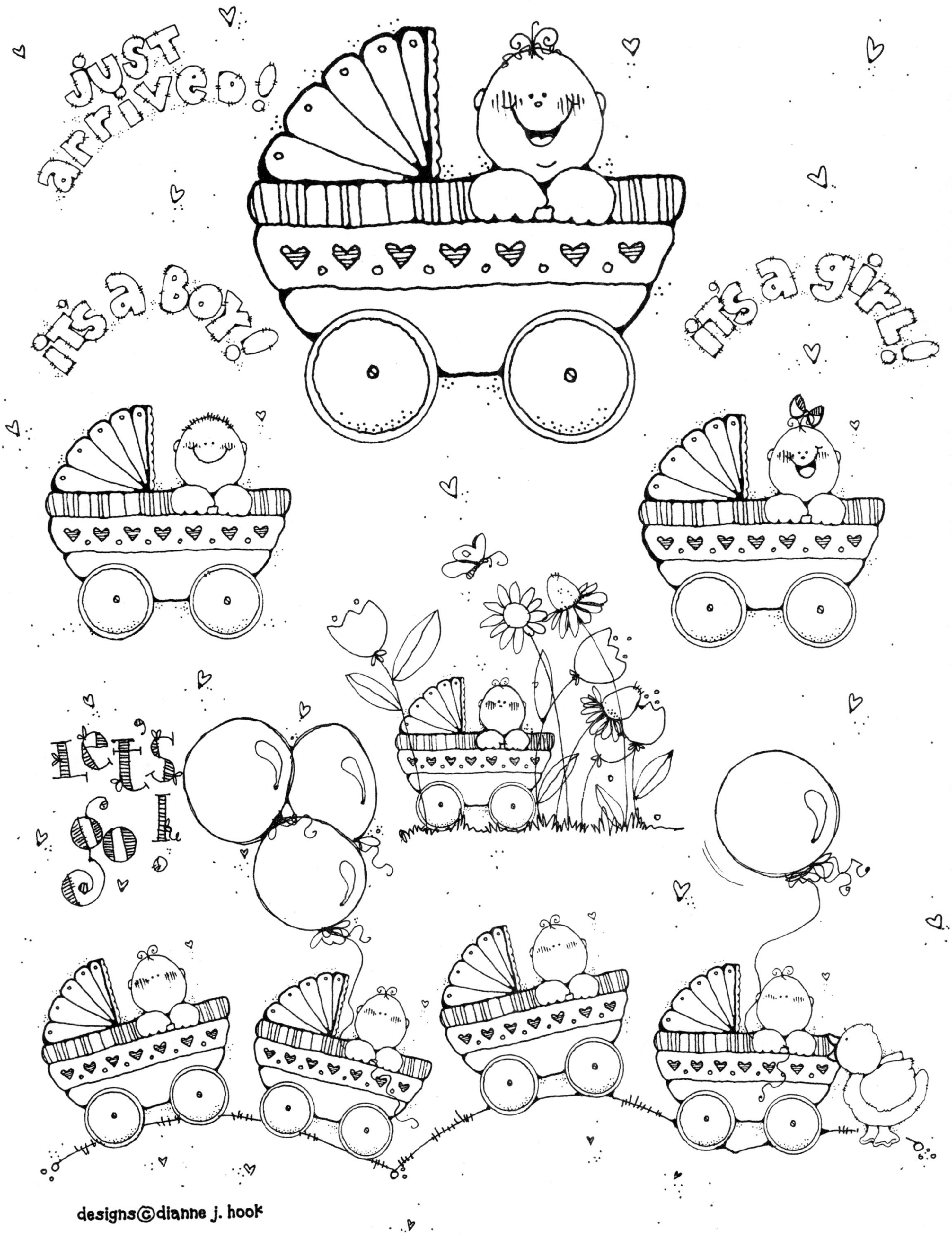
just arrived!
it's a boy!
it's a girl!
let's go!

MY favorite foods...

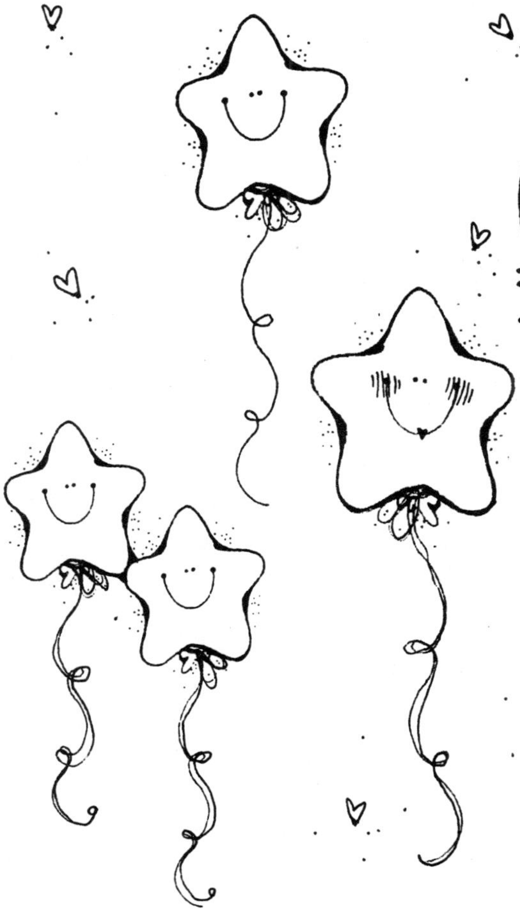

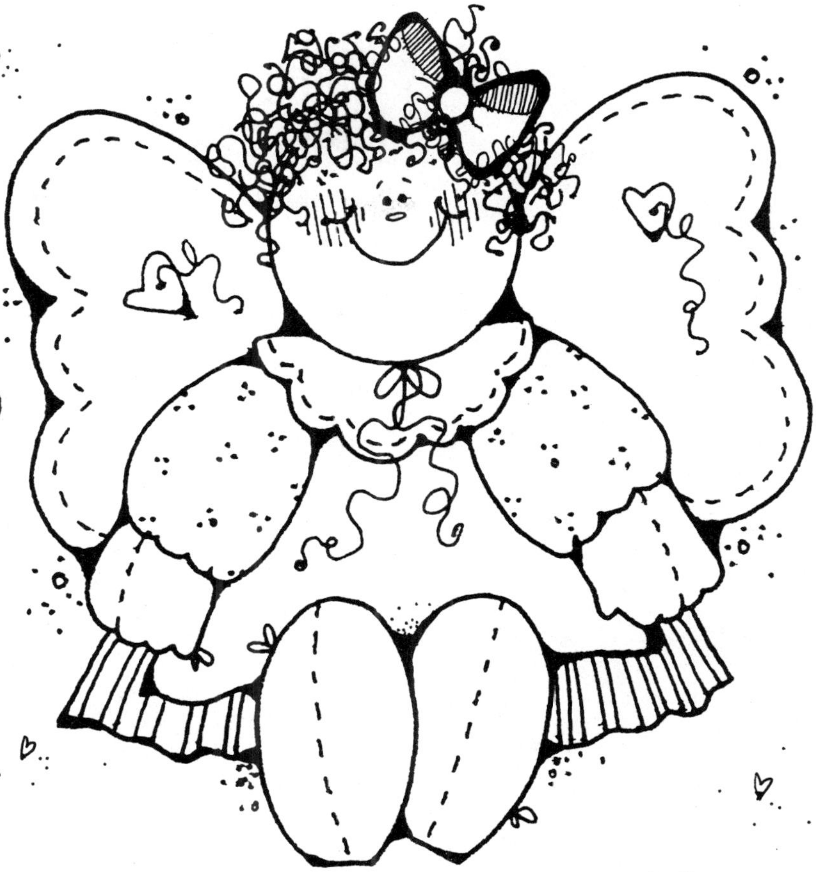

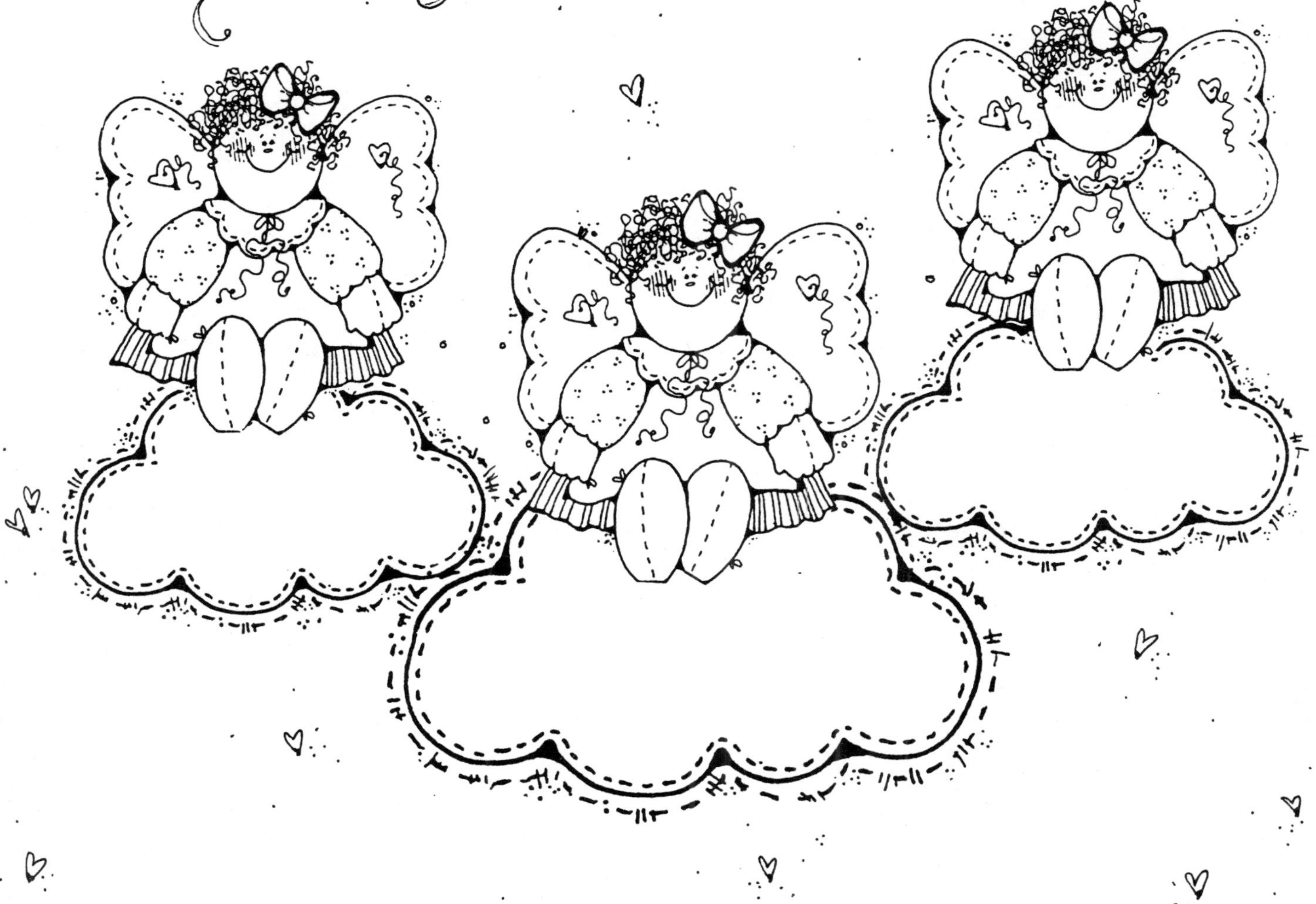

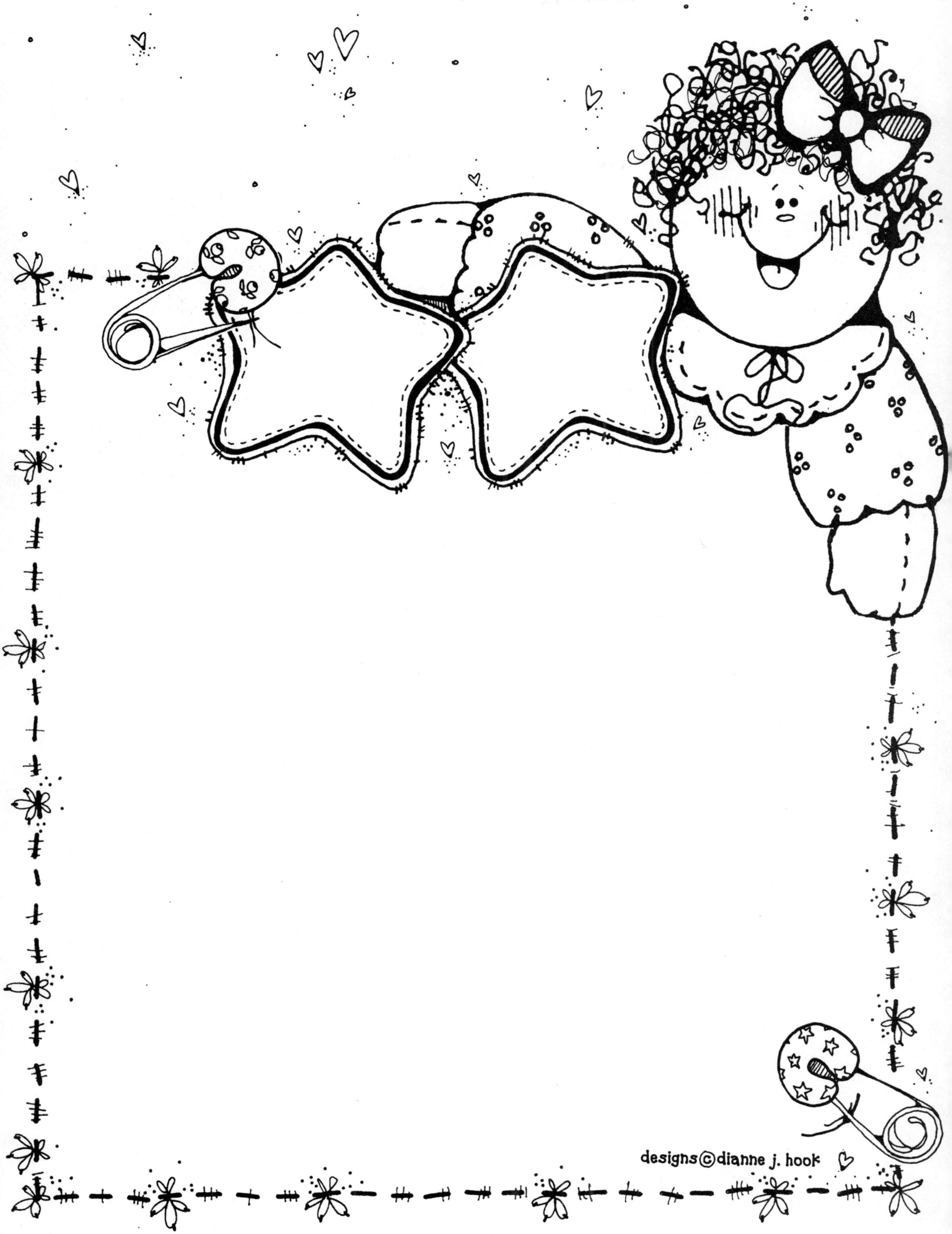

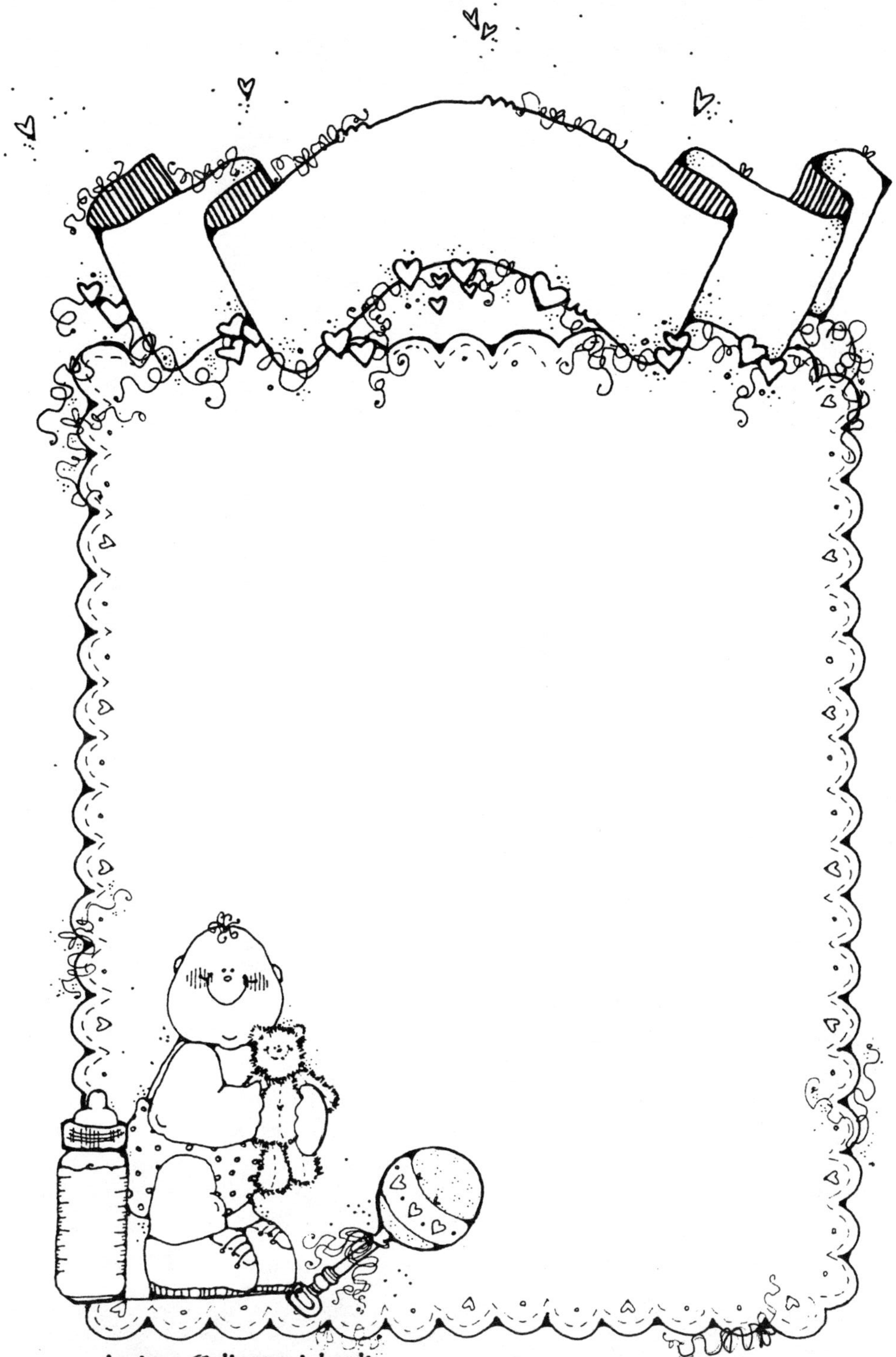

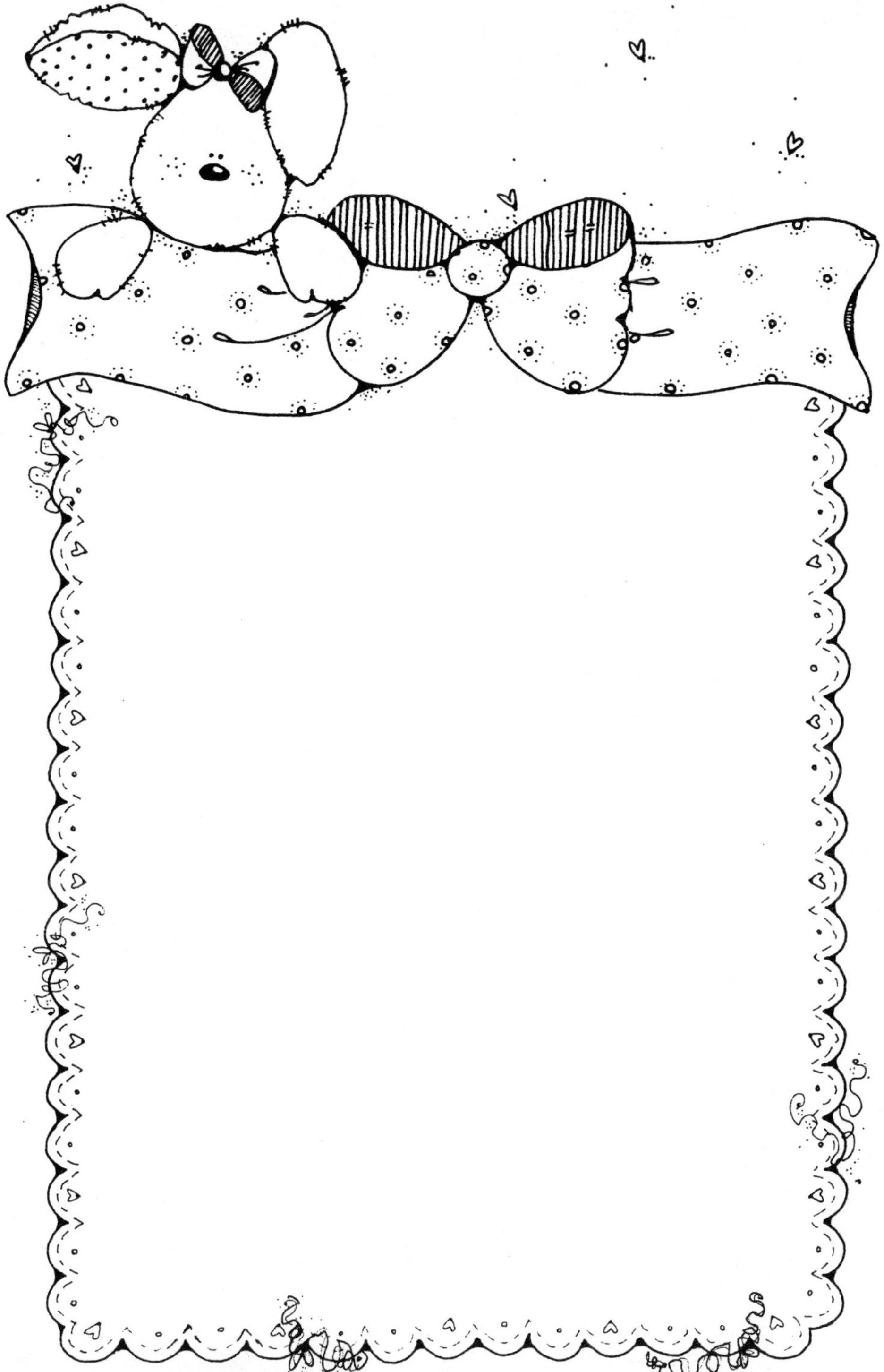

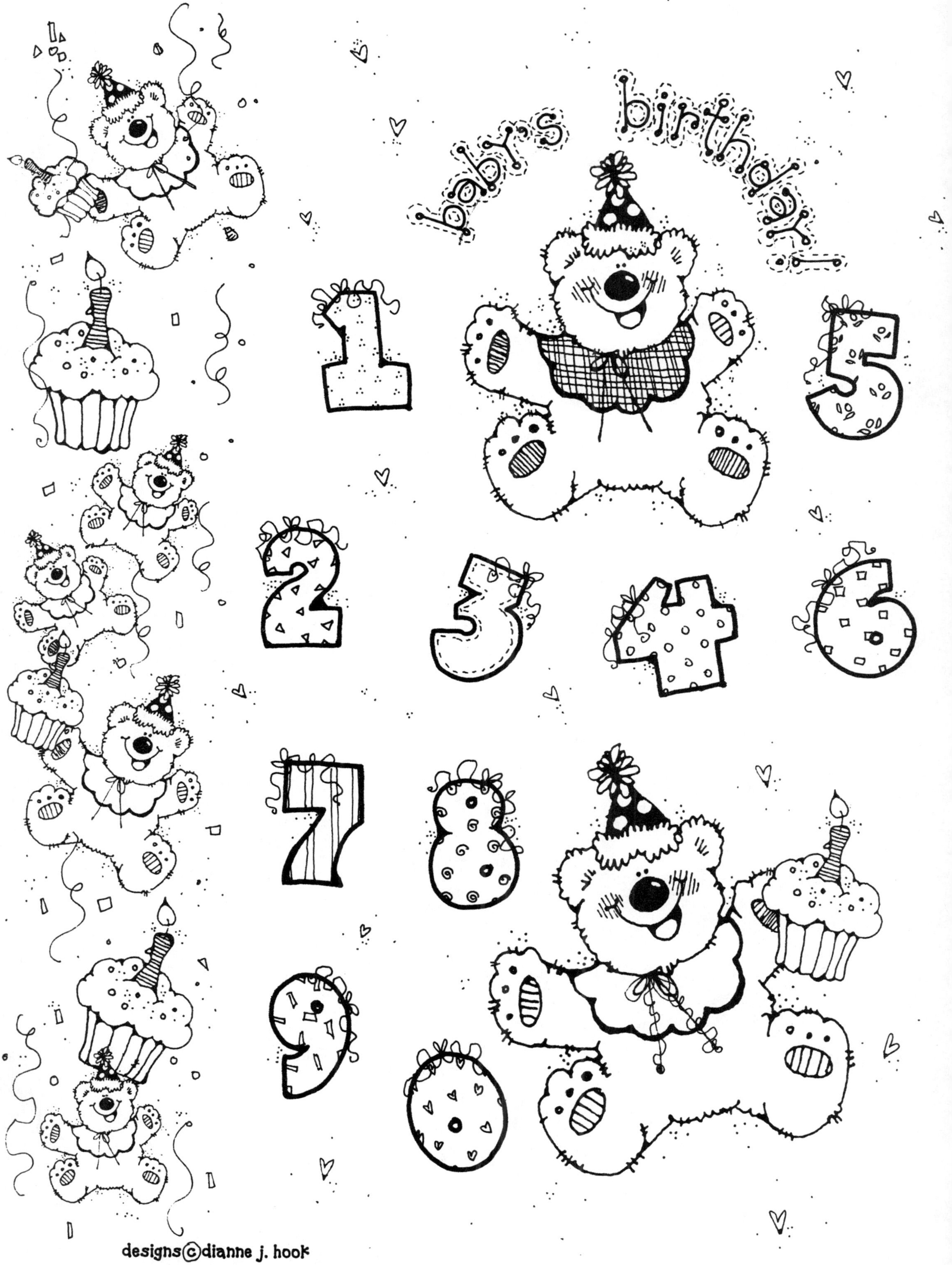

designs©dianne j. hook

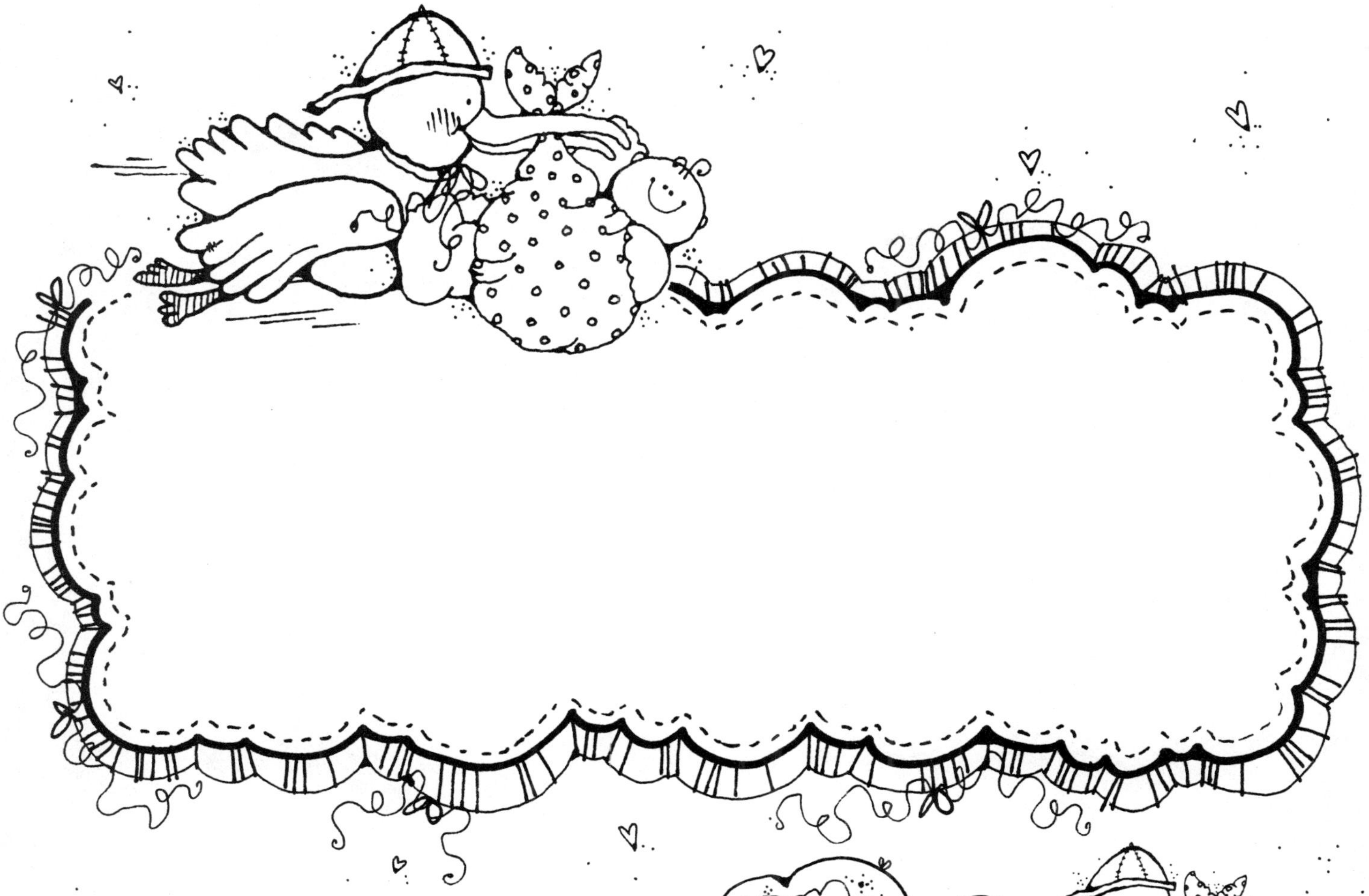

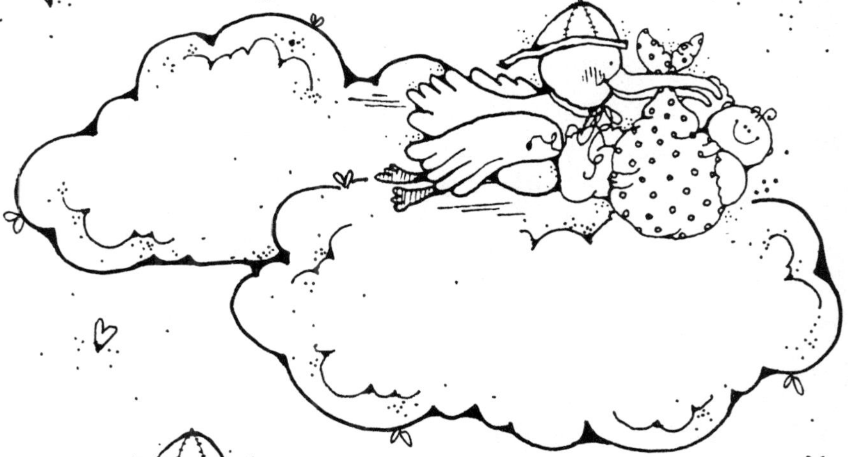

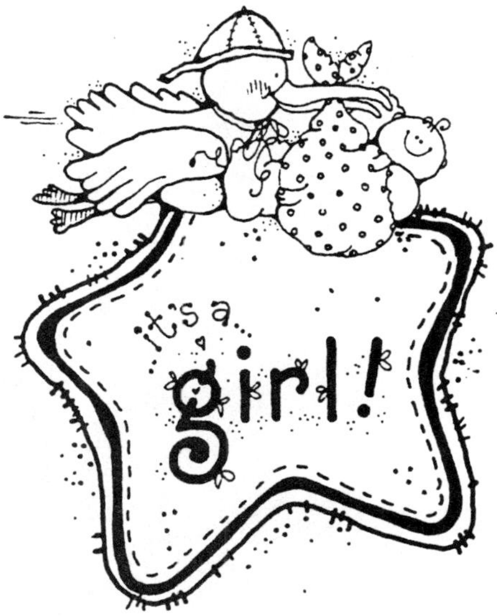

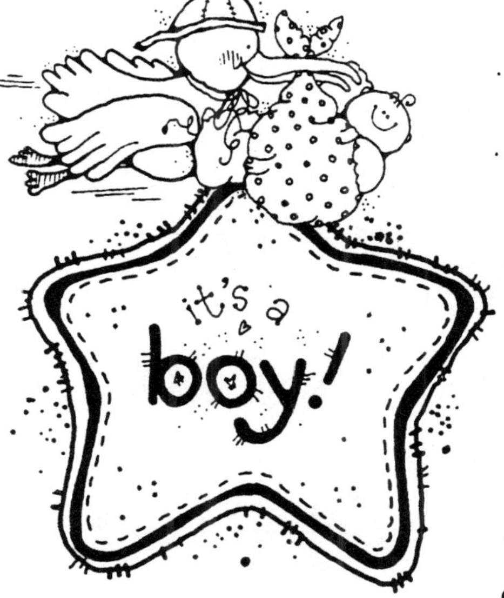

it's a
girl!

it's a
boy!

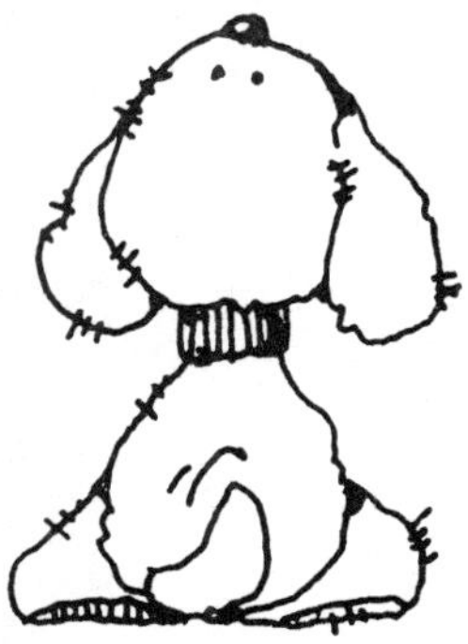

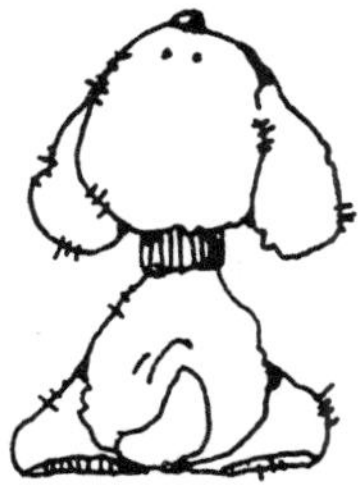

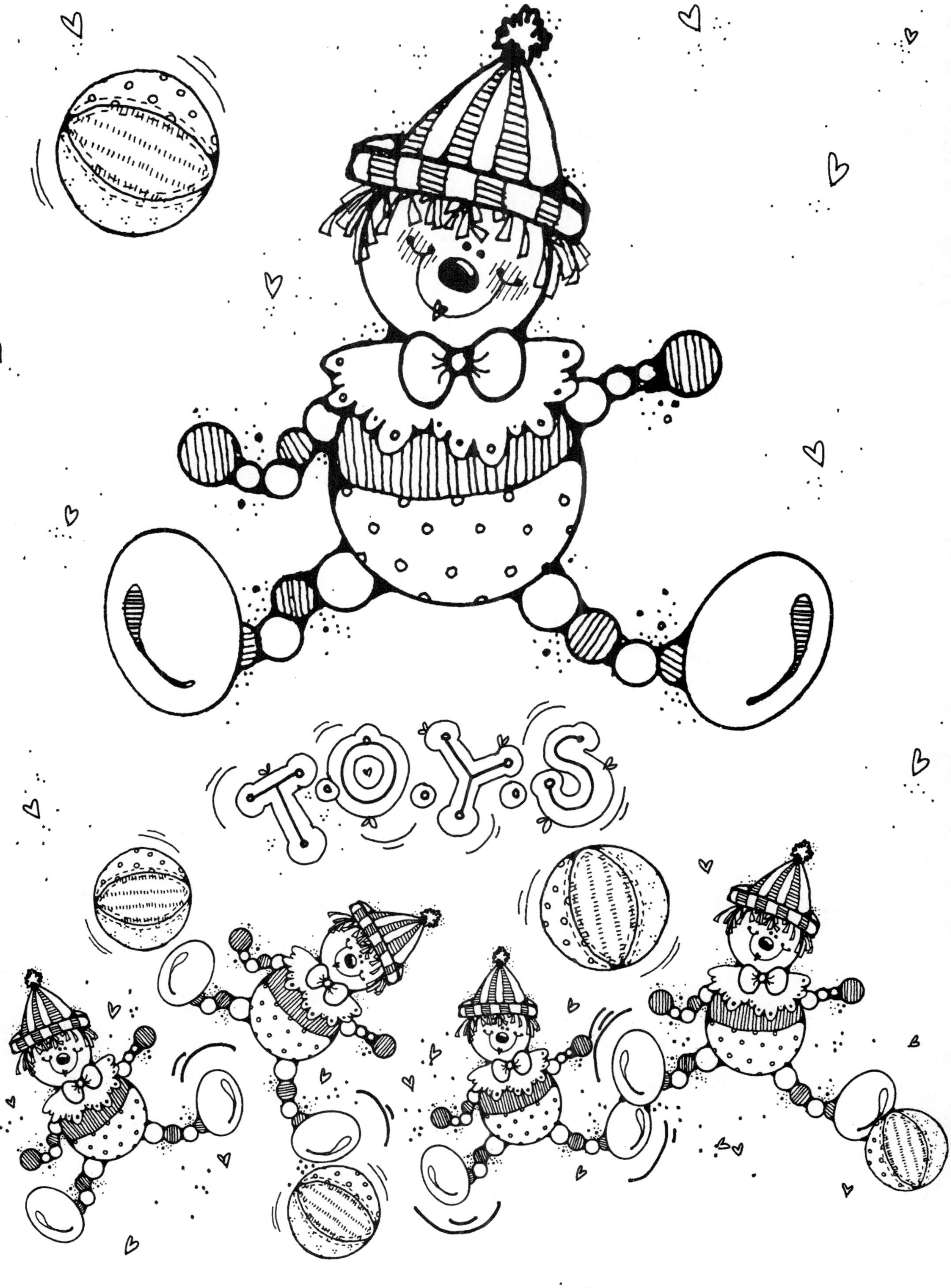
T.O.Y.S

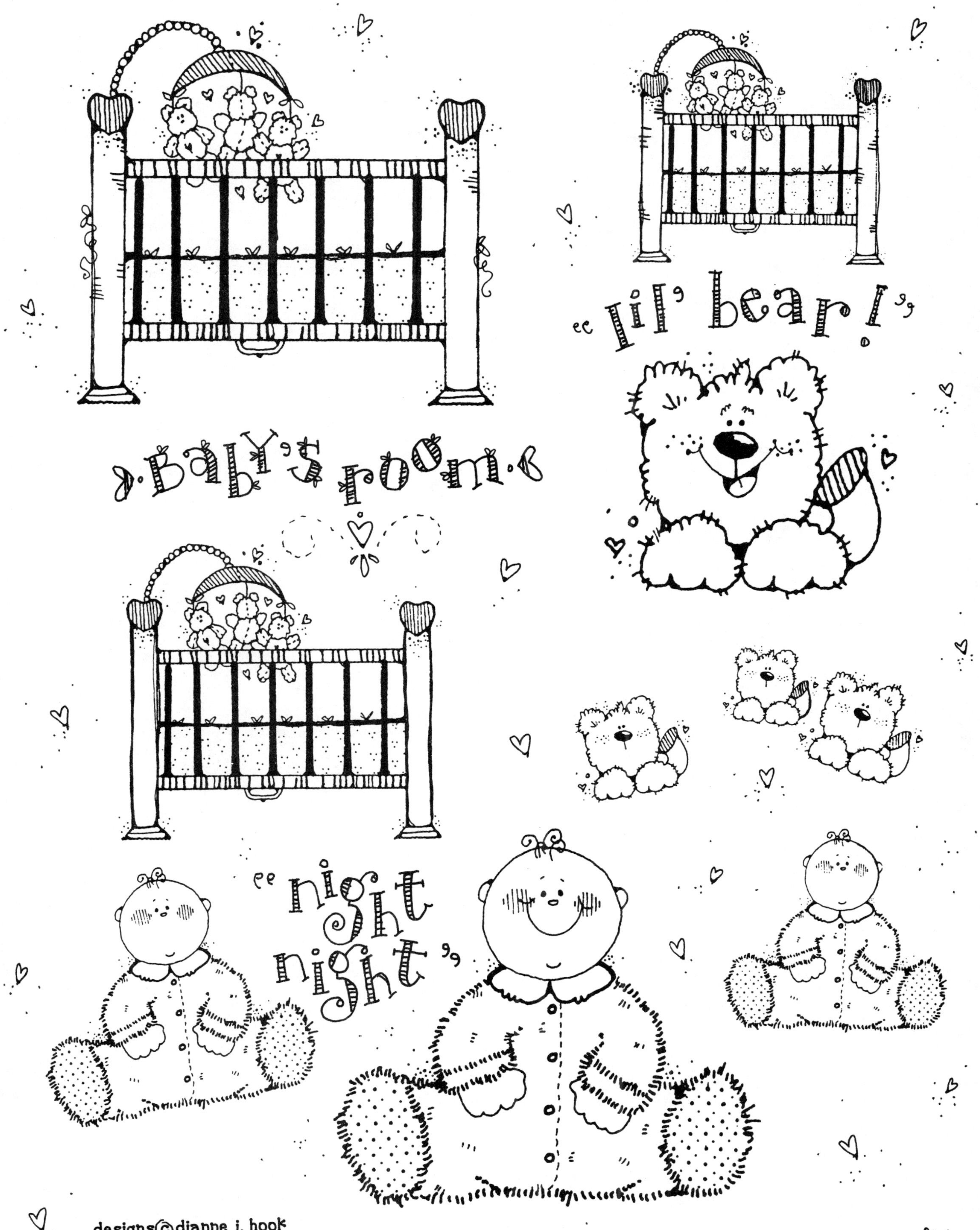

designs © dianne j. hook

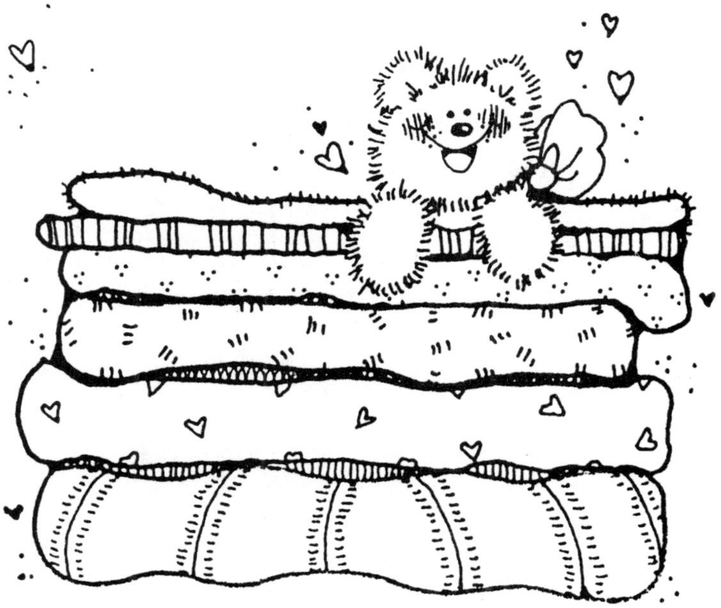

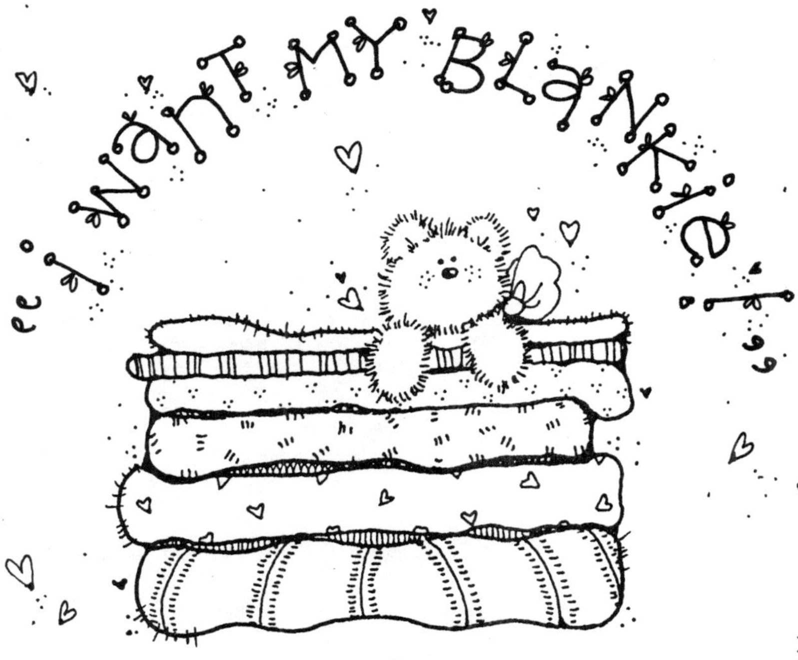
"I WANT MY BLANKIE!"

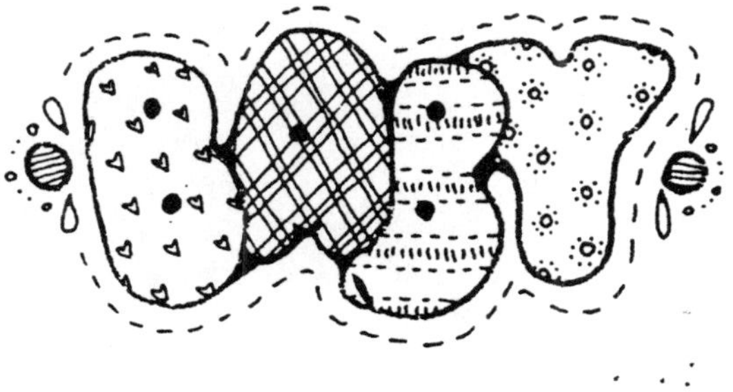
BABY

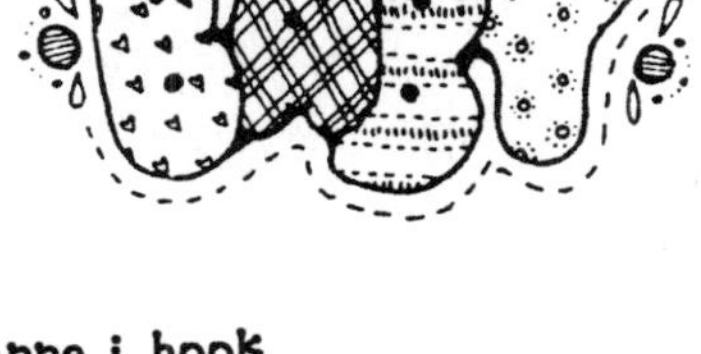
BABY

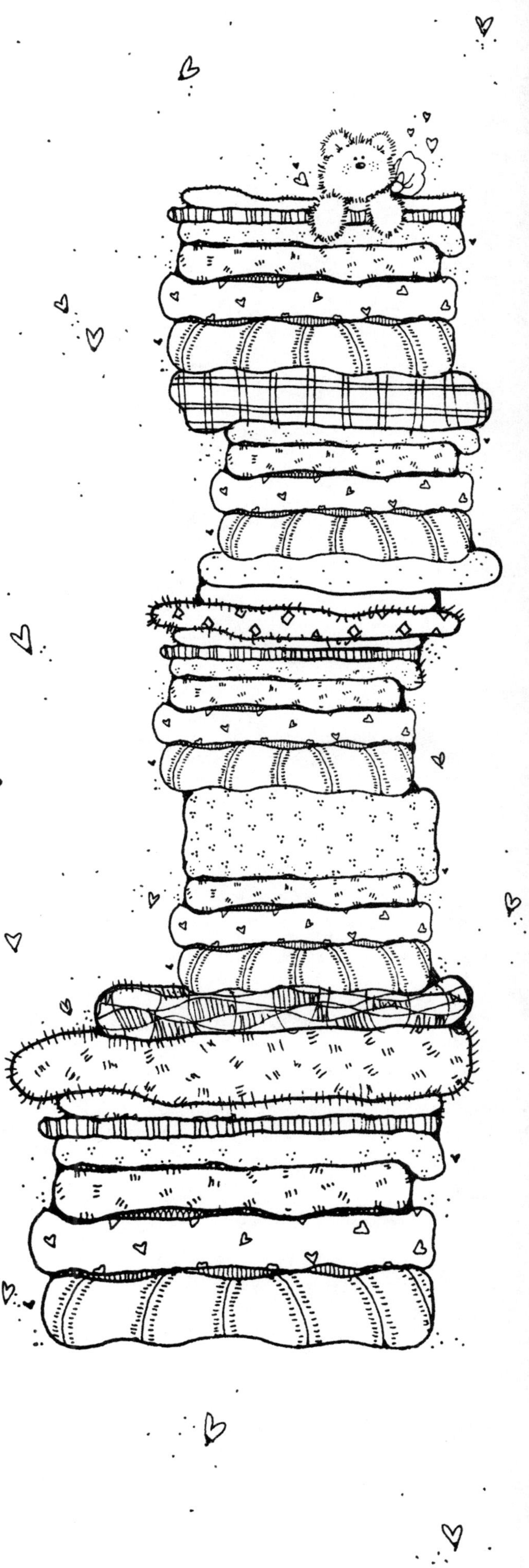

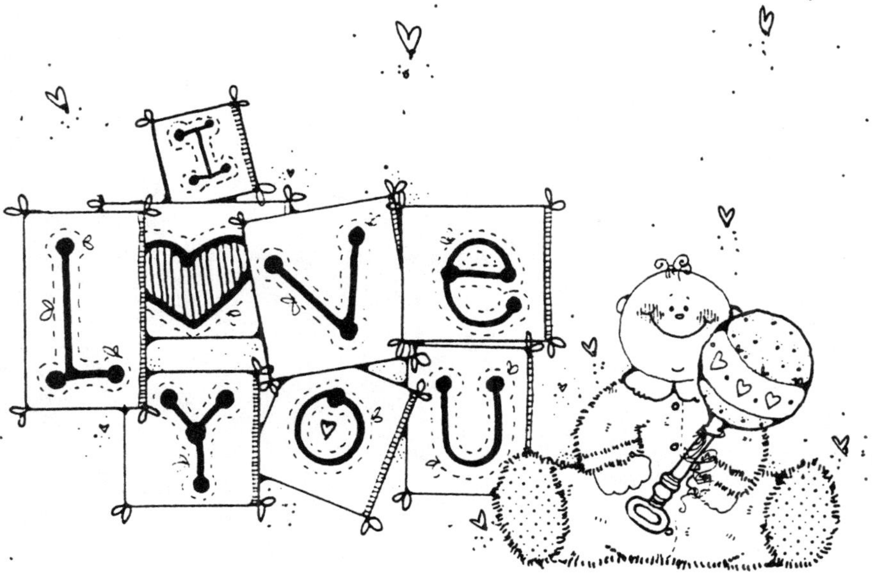
I
L Ve
YOU

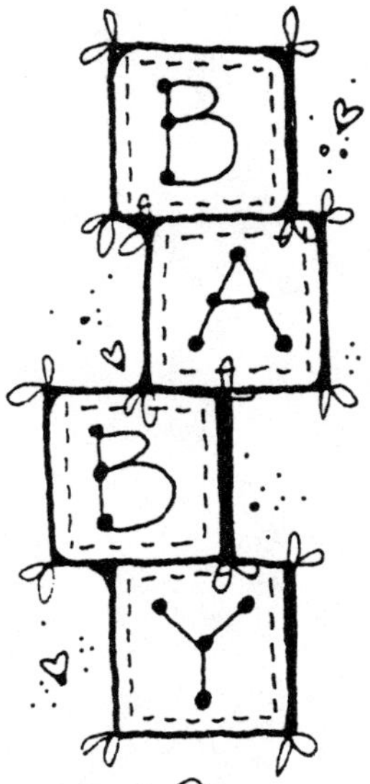
B
A
B
Y

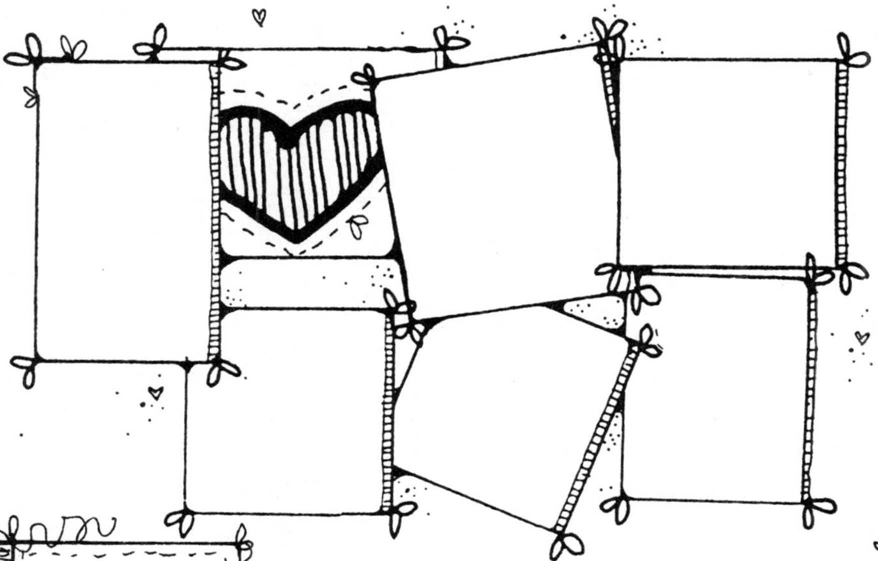

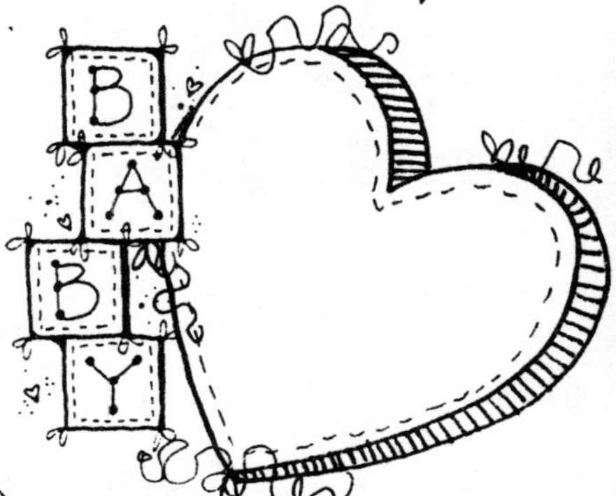
B
A
B
Y

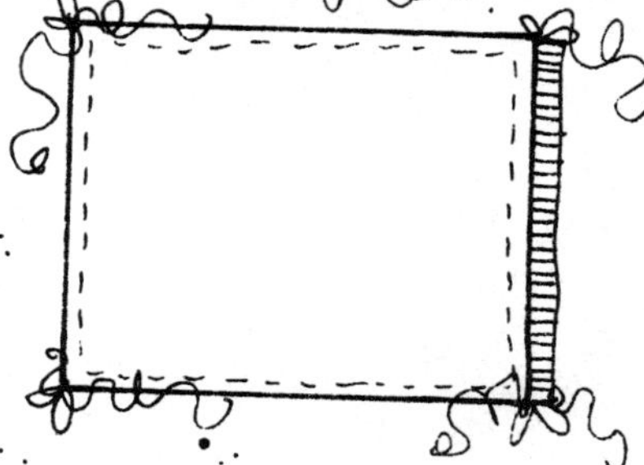

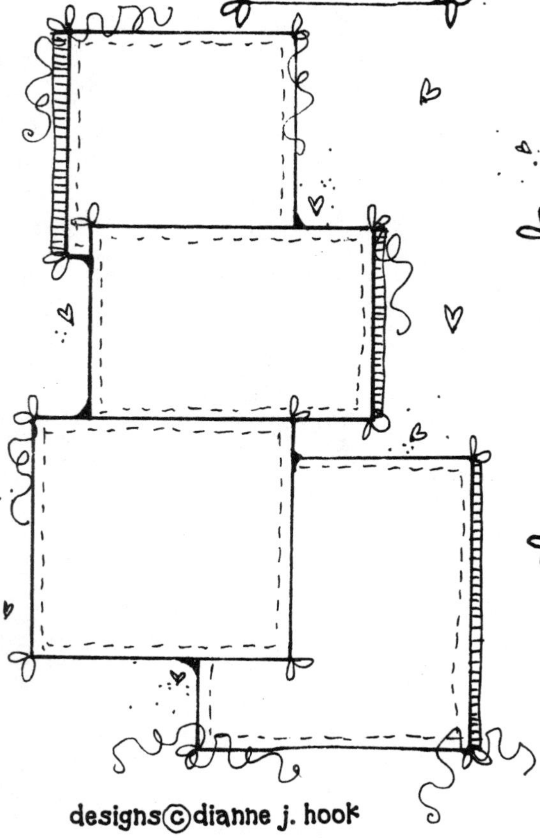

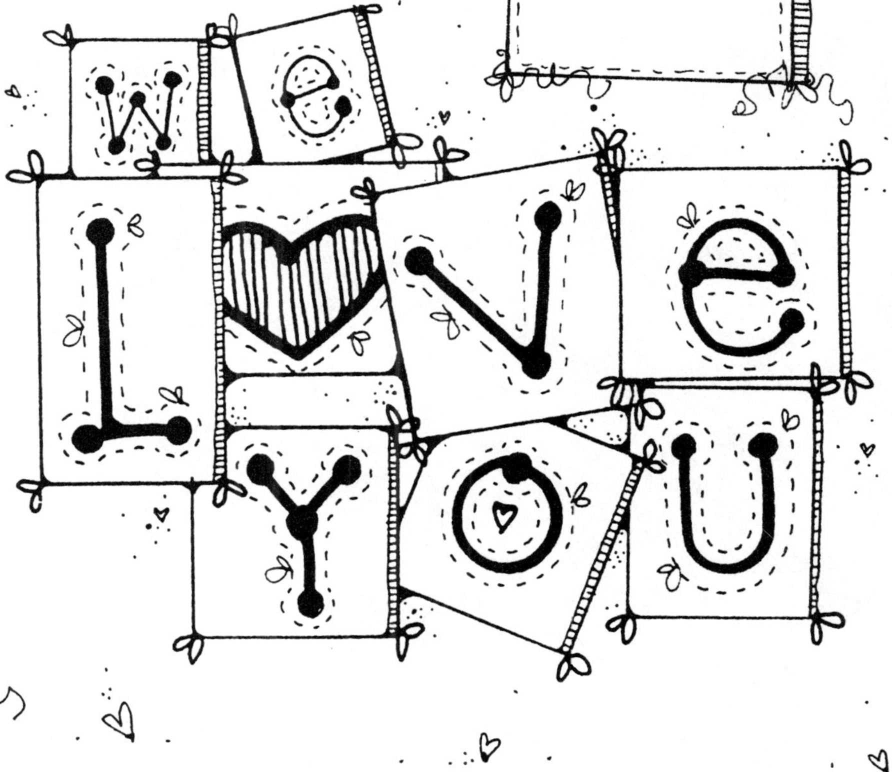
We
L Ve
YOU

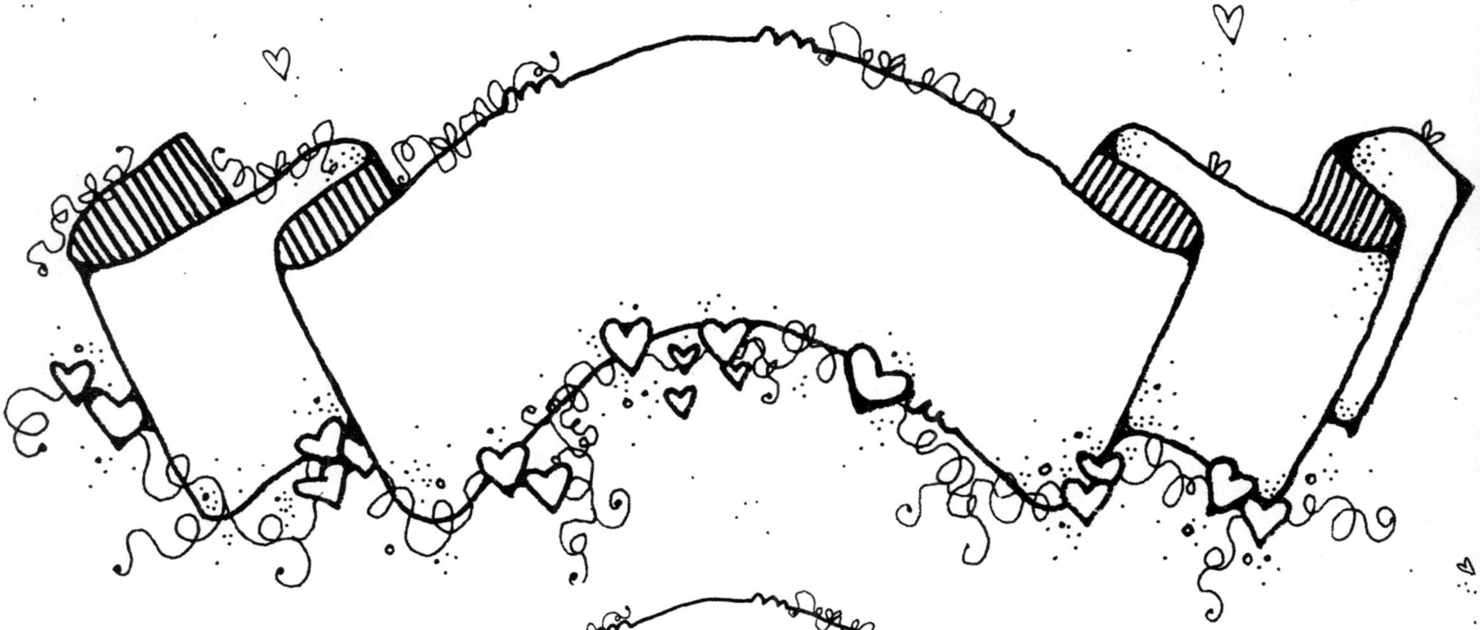

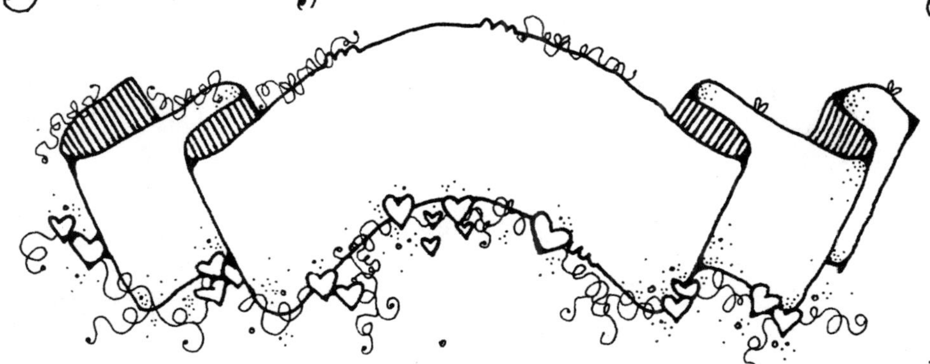

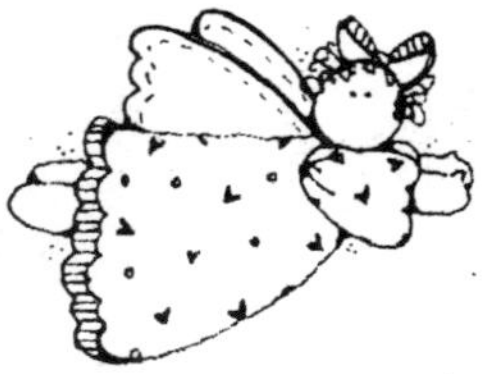

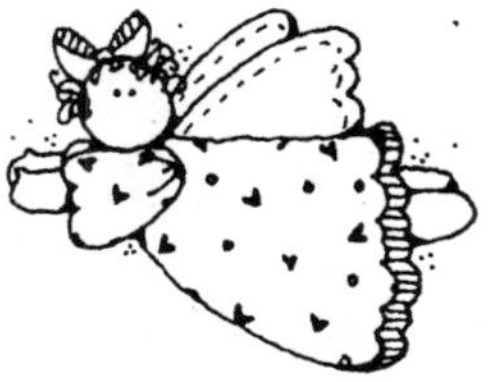

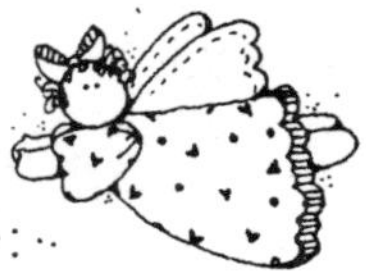

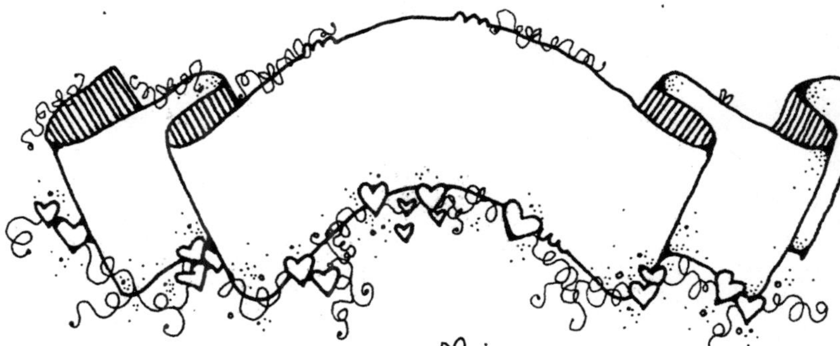

Babies are little angels

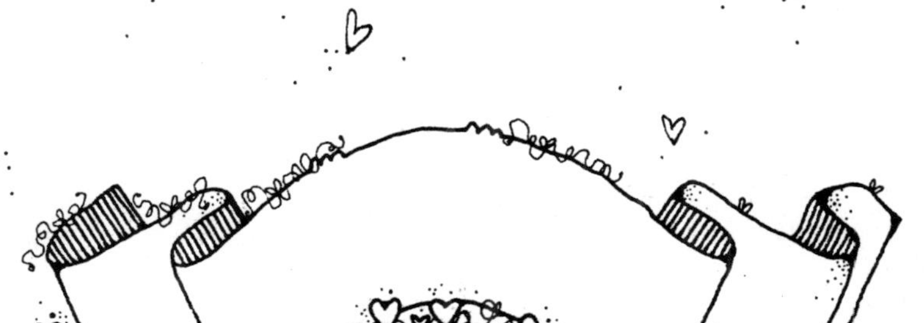

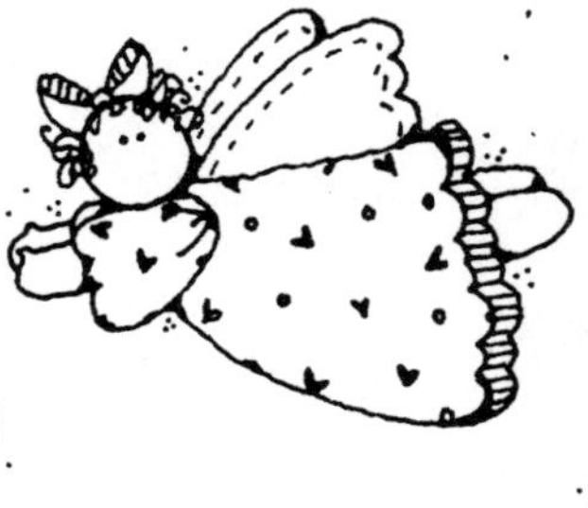

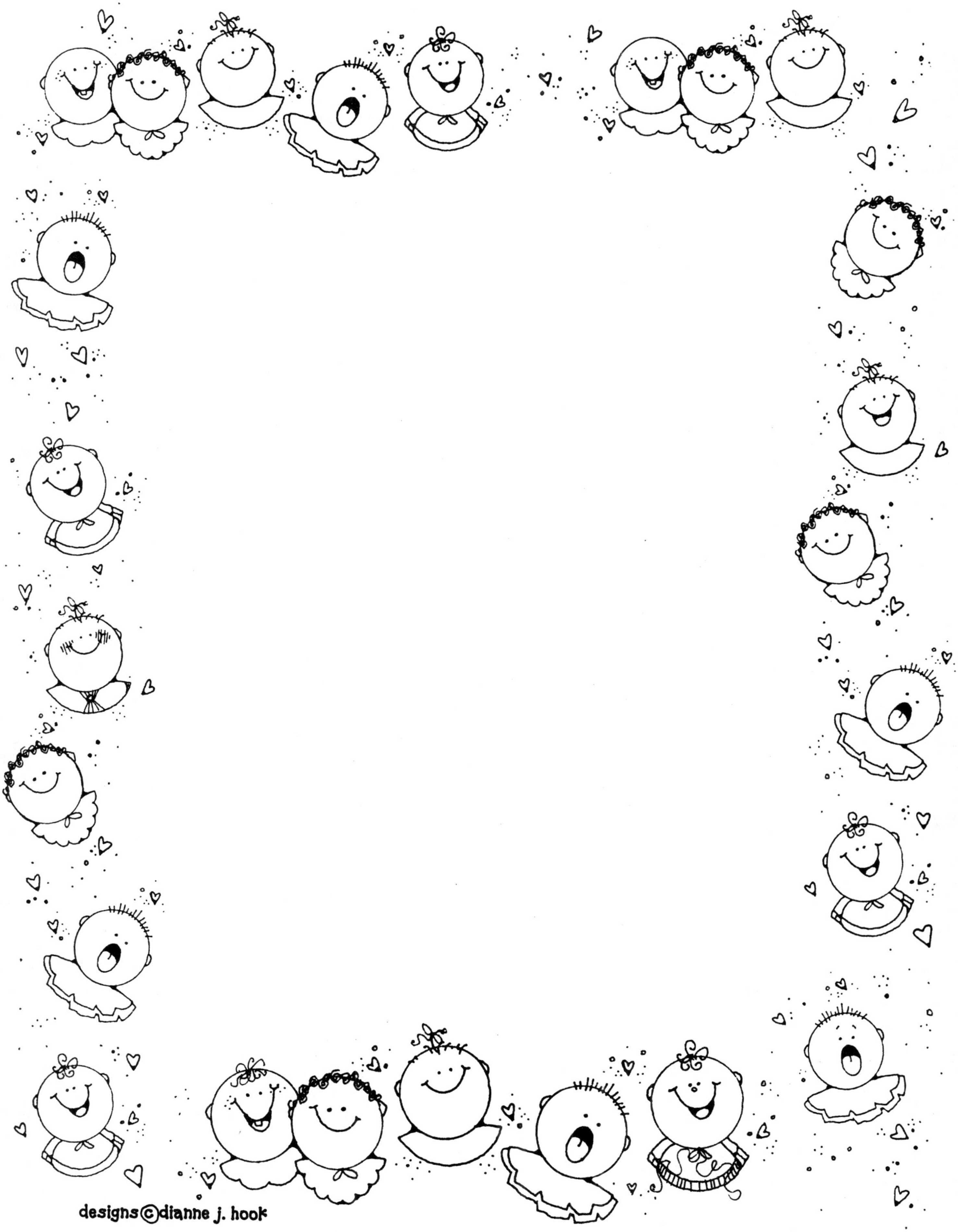

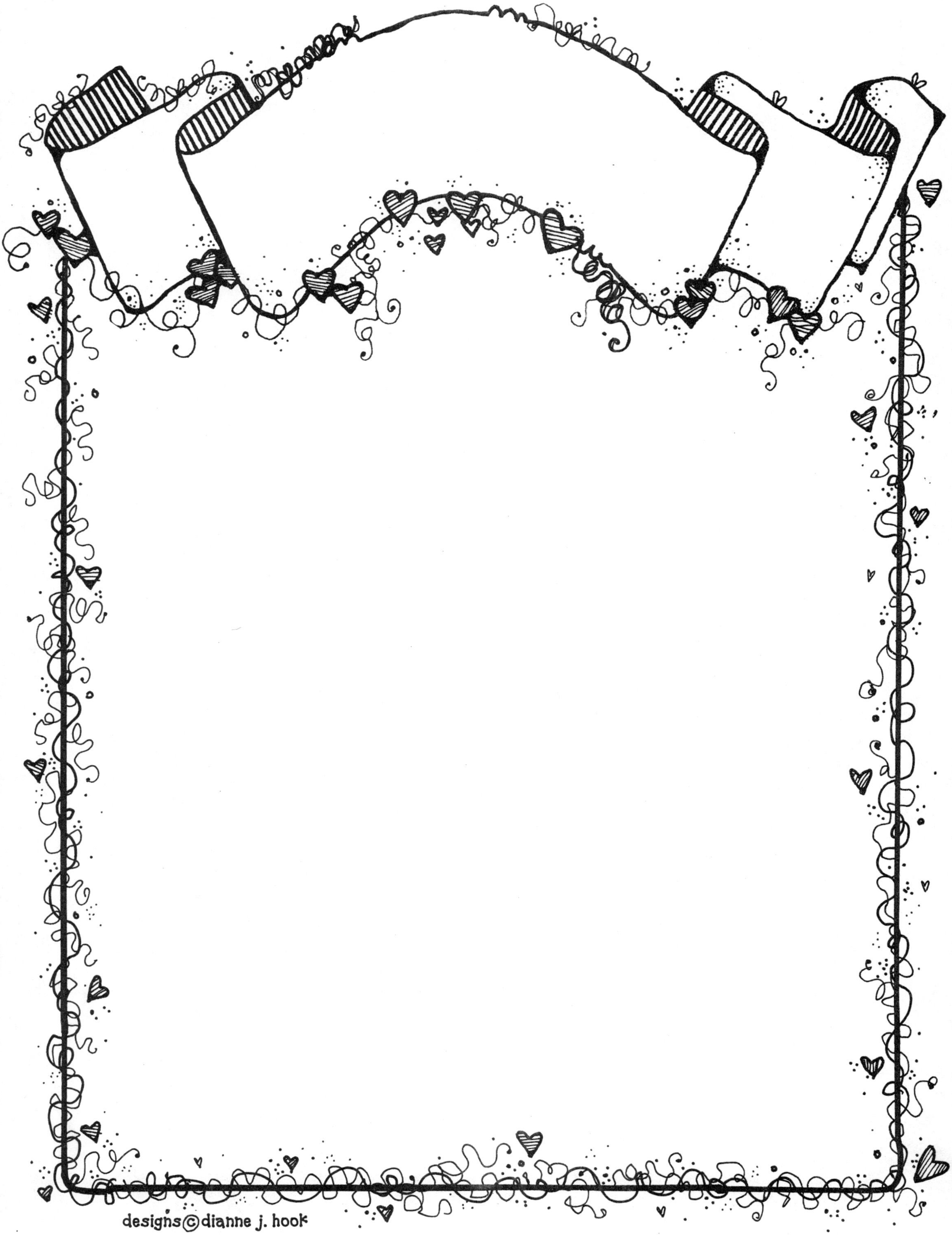

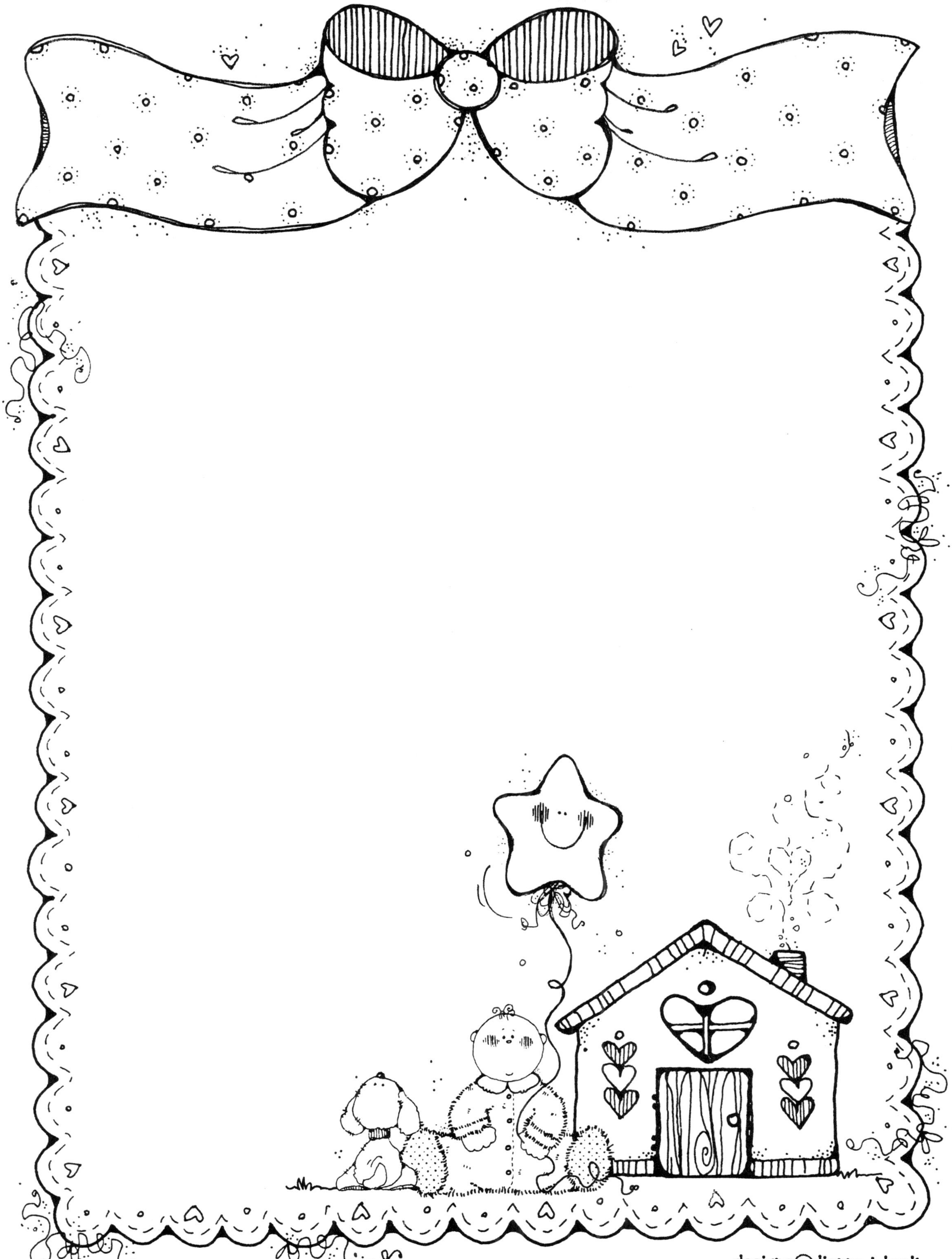

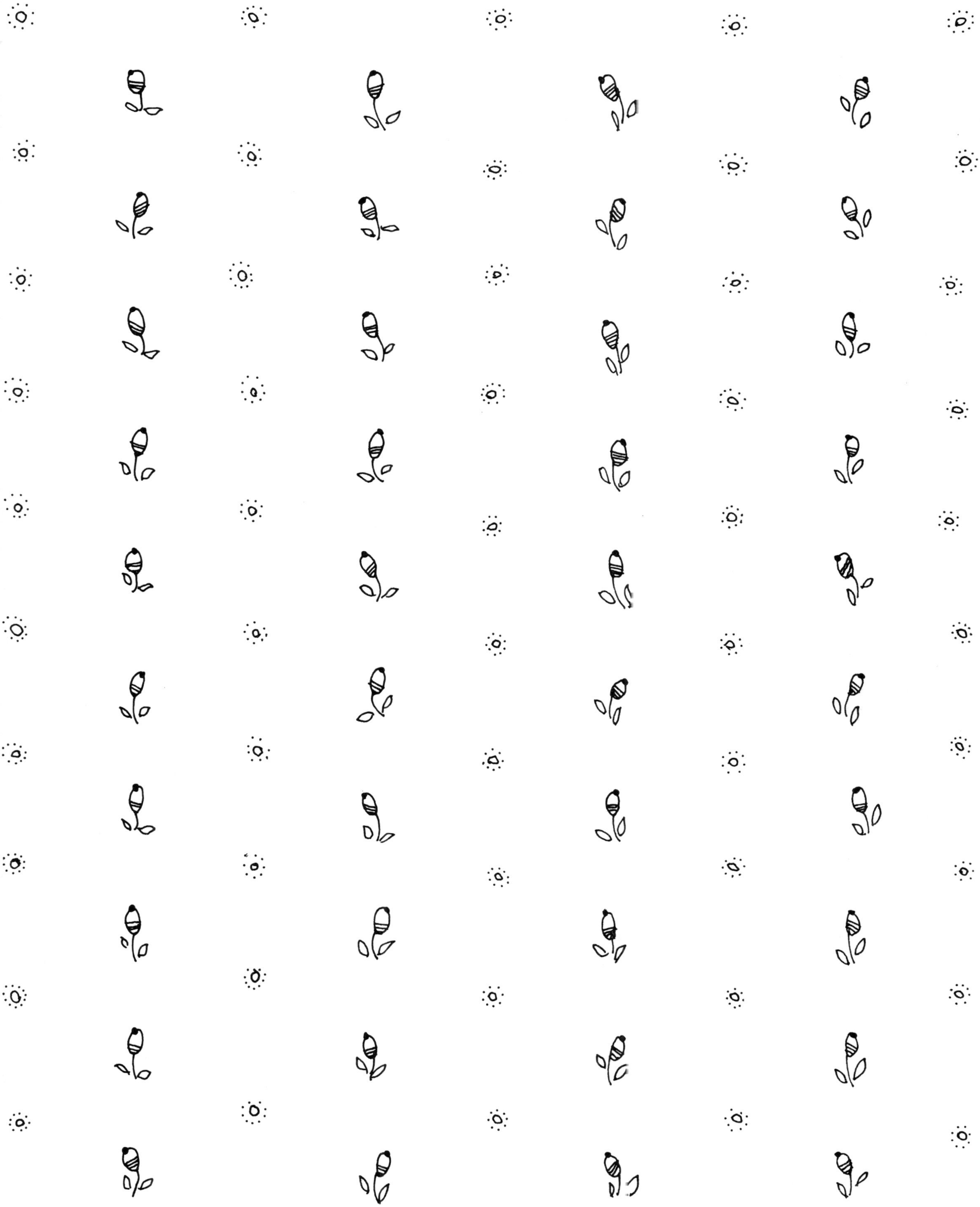

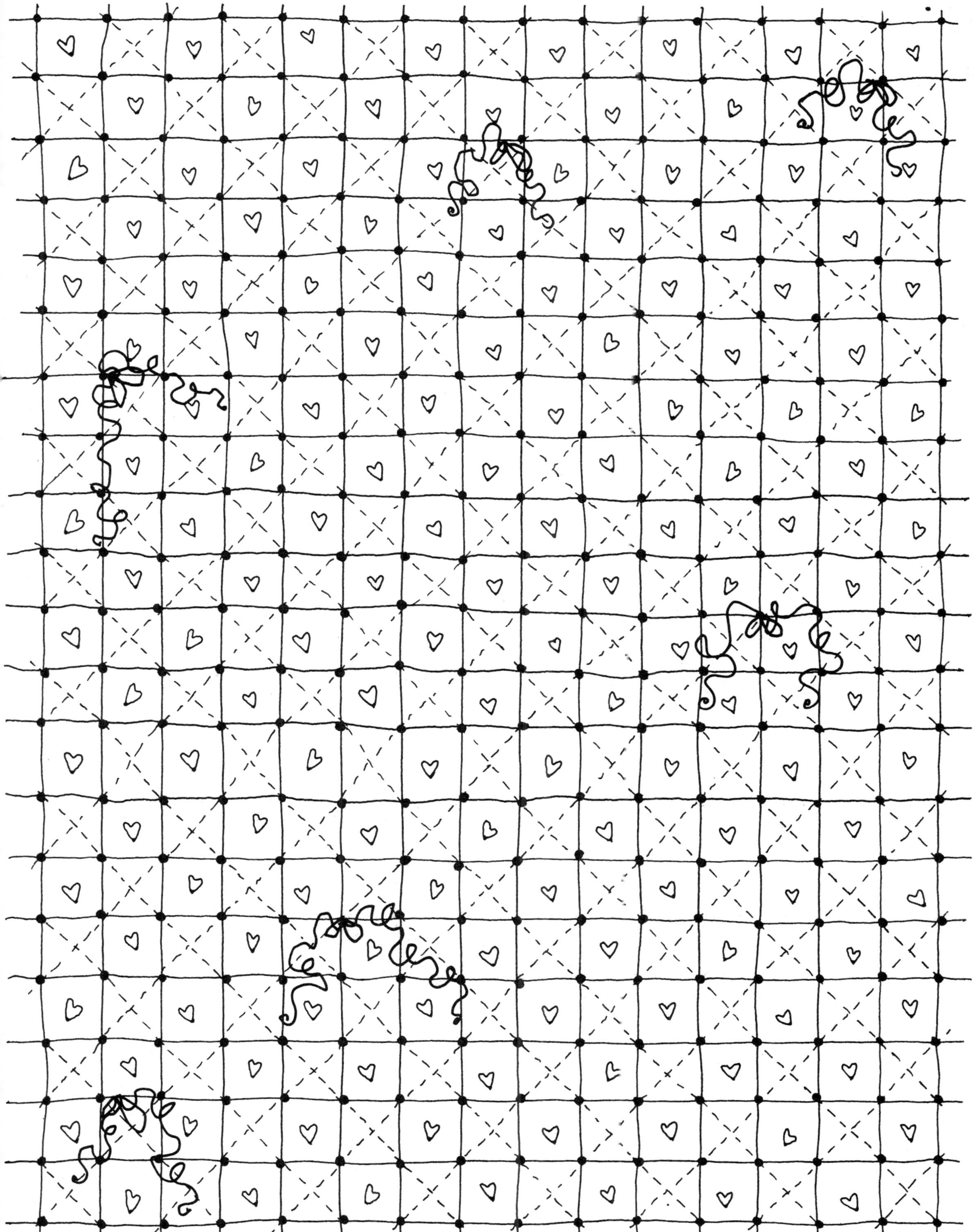

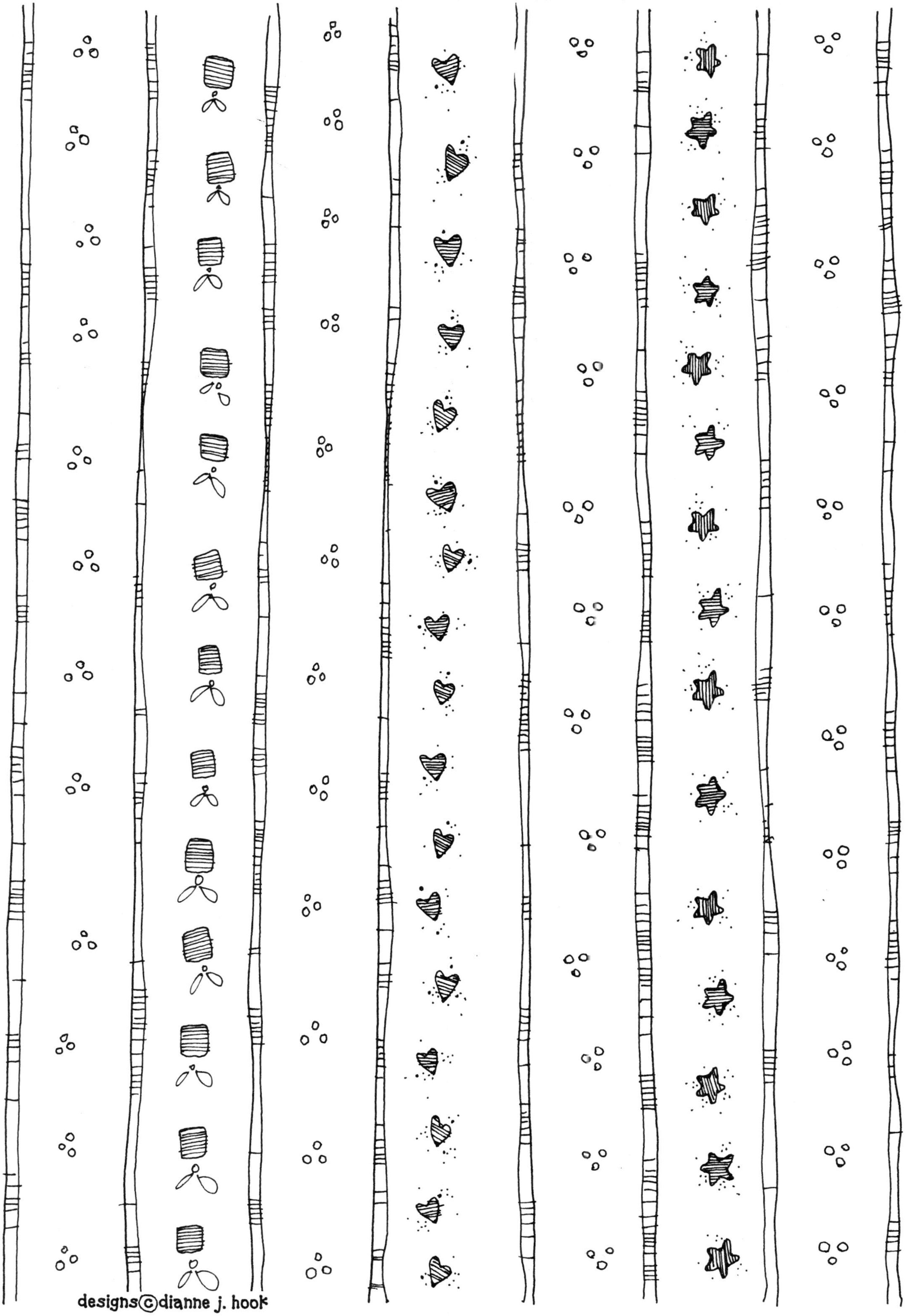

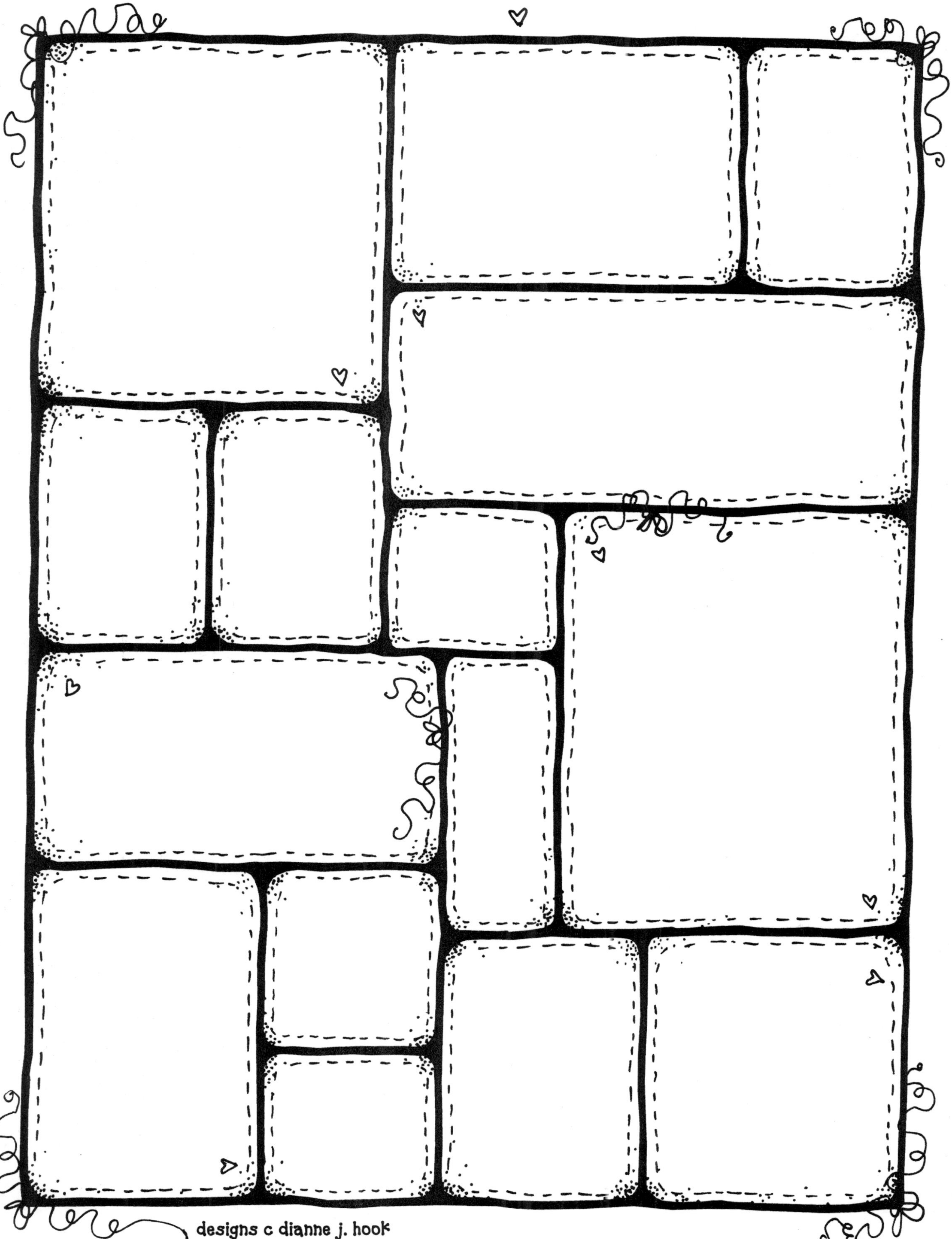

designs c dianne j. hook

Lettering Guide for DJ Chunky

A a B b C c D d

E e F f G g H h I

i J j K k L l

M m N n O o P p

Q q R r S s T t

U u V v W w X x

Y y Z z

? ! & ...

This is a sweet little lettering style for doing baby projects! If you are using a light table as you create different headings and titles for your projects, don't forget to be extra creative and try different sizes, colors, and styles of pens and markers. Try little stitching lines around the edges of the letter too, for that country quilted effect. This lettering style is also available for your computer on our DAZZLE DAZE software, along with four other fonts that you will love in personalizing!